Praise for *Dogs and the Women Who Love Them* by Allen & Linda Anderson

"The rescuing works both ways again in Allen and Linda Andersons' collection as canines who've suffered abuse, neglect, or misfortune seek and comfort humans who've endured the same."

— Karen Holt, *O: The Oprah Magazine*

"When asked, 'Betty, you never remarried! How can you live alone?' my answer is simple: my golden retriever, Pontiac, is my saving grace."

— Betty White, actress and author

"This book is for all dog lovers, and for those who wish to better understand the human-animal bond. It's an inspiring read and will make you want to hug your best friend!"

— Patrick McDonnell, creator of *MUTTS*

"These heartwarming stories of dogs and the women who love them solidify the fact that the animal-human bond is so unique and necessary for enhancing one's life. You'll find a bit of yourself in each tale."

— Vanessa Williams, actress and singer

"Whether you're a 'normal' dog mom, a psycho dog mom…or somewhere in between, this book will open your heart, warm your soul, and make you proud to be a dog-loving woman."

— from the foreword by Rory Freedman

"Perhaps because my older sister was a collie, I am never more myself than when in the presence of a dog. Kudos to Allen and Linda for sharing the myriad ways dogs bring joy, healing, and gratitude into our lives."

— Wendie Malick, actor and advocate

"Packed with vivid characters, zippy anecdotes and memorable moments, *Dogs and the Women Who Love Them* blends spirit and spunk into absorbing first-person narratives that inspire, empower, enlighten and have you begging for more."

— Ranny Green, former president of the Dog Writers Association of America

Animals and the Kids Who Love Them

Also by Allen and Linda Anderson

Angel Animals: Divine Messengers of Miracles

Angel Animals Book of Inspiration:
Divine Messengers of Wisdom and Compassion

Angel Cats: Divine Messengers of Comfort

Angel Dogs: Divine Messengers of Love

Angel Dogs with a Mission:
Divine Messengers in Service to All Life

Angel Horses: Divine Messengers of Hope

Dogs and the Women Who Love Them:
Extraordinary True Stories of Loyalty, Healing & Inspiration

Horses with a Mission:
Extraordinary True Stories of Equine Service

Rainbows and Bridges: An Animal Companion Memorial Kit

Rescued: Saving Animals from Disaster

Saying Goodbye to Your Angel Animals:
Finding Comfort After Losing Your Pet

Animals and the Kids Who Love Them

Extraordinary True Stories of Hope, Healing, and Compassion

Allen & Linda Anderson

Foreword by American Humane Association's president and
CEO Robin R. Ganzert, PhD, and board member Steve Dale

New World Library
Novato, California

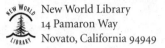 New World Library
14 Pamaron Way
Novato, California 94949

Text design by Tona Pearce Myers

Library of Congress Cataloging-in-Publication Data
Anderson, Allen, date.
 Animals and the kids who love them : extraordinary true stories of hope, healing, and compassion / Allen and Linda Anderson ; foreword by Robin R. Ganzert and Steve Dale.
  p.   cm.
Includes bibliographical references.
ISBN 978-1-57731-959-7 (pbk. : alk. paper)
1. Pets—Anecdotes. 2. Pets—Psychological aspects—Anecdotes. 3. Children and animals—Anecdotes. 4. Human-animal relationships—Anecdotes. 5. Children—Biography—Anecdotes. 6. Pet owners—Biography—Anecdotes. 7. Hope—Anecdotes. 8. Healing—Anecdotes. 9. Compassion—Anecdotes. I. Anderson, Linda C., date. II. Title.
 SF416.A53 2011
 636.088'7—dc23   2011030538

First printing, November 2011
ISBN 978-1-57731-959-7
Printed in the United States on 100% postconsumer-waste recycled paper

𝖌 New World Library is a proud member of the Green Press Initiative.

10 9 8 7 6 5 4 3 2 1

Contents

Part One. Hope

Part Two. Healing

Part Three. Compassion

Foreword

....

Robin R. Ganzert, PhD, and Steve Dale

For as long as people have organized themselves into tribes, clans, communities, city-states, and nations, animals have been a part of their story. For example, in ancient Greece, Aesop used animals as the characters in fables that we still tell our children today. Traditional Navajo legends are replete with the exploits of the trickster Coyote. And who hasn't been thrilled by the adventures of the hero dog Rin Tin Tin or one of his many Hollywood cousins?

In *Animals and the Kids Who Love Them*, we're constantly reminded of the strength, depth, and durability of the human-animal bond. We're especially touched by how powerful this bond is when it comes to the connection with children. Within these pages you'll read real-life stories that will make you chuckle, well up with tears, or just sit and ponder in amazement. Perhaps as remarkable as the stories themselves is the diversity of animals they include. We all know someone who has loved and been comforted by a cat, dog, or horse; here we meet turtles, llamas, baby chicks, rabbits, guinea pigs, and even a turkey.

At the heart of these remarkable stories is the message that there is no such thing as "beyond hope." Life has put seemingly insurmountable obstacles in the way of many of these children. But through the unconditional love and sympathetic patience of animal companions, they persevere. This lesson is one we learn and relearn every day at American Humane Association. As the only national organization with the mission of safeguarding and lifting up the lives of both children and animals, sometimes we can feel as if we are on the front lines of heartbreak. Yet for every act of unspeakable cruelty we encounter that threatens to crush our spirit, a thousand examples of compassion, caring, and hope rush in to refresh and renew our determination.

Although at American Humane Association we intuitively understand the power of the human-animal bond — and experience it hundreds of times a day — we also know that for that bond to be truly harnessed and its possibilities realized, there must be a scientific understanding of what it is and how it works. In just one example, beginning in 2011 American Humane Association is leading a major nationwide study of the effect of therapy animals on the treatment of children with cancer. In this landmark project, researchers will examine the medical, behavioral, and mental health benefits of animal-assisted therapy to quantify its effects on patients and their families. This is just one of the interconnected pillars of research, policy, and programs on which American Humane Association's work is built. Since 1877, we have been at the forefront of every major effort in this country to change laws and shape attitudes to better protect the most vulnerable among us. In communities around the nation, American Humane Association–led initiatives are creating safe places in which children and animals can grow up, thrive, and reach their full potential.

Dr. Robin Ganzert and Gatsby

Advocacy, action, and knowledge of the kind pioneered by American Humane Association are critical components in help-

ing ensure that our world is the humane, compassion-ate place people from every culture, background, and belief system strive every day to build. However in the end it is the inspiring stories of the magic that happens when people and animals connect at a deep and interpersonal level — stories like the ones so poi-gnantly told in this book — that will always serve as the blueprint for what we want that world to look

Steve Dale and his late pets
*Lucy the dog and Ringo the cat**

like. With tales that reveal new meaning and inspire new hope on each rereading, *Animals and the Kids Who Love Them* will be a nightstand staple in our homes. We hope it brightens yours as well.

— Robin R. Ganzert, PhD, president and CEO
of American Humane Association, and
Steve Dale, CABC, syndicated columnist,
radio host of *Steve Dale's Pet World*, and
American Humane Association board member
and national ambassador

* Ringo's Feline Infectious Peritonitis (FIP) inspired the Bria Fund at the Winn Feline Foundation to support FIP studies (www.winnfelinehealth .org/pages/briafund.html). Lucy's animal-assisted therapy work inspired the Lucy Fund at American Humane Association (http://americanhumane blog.org/2011/05/lucy-funny-little-dog-she-lived-to-put-smiles-on-faces/).

Introduction

Allen and Linda Anderson

In 1869, twelve-year-old Emily recorded costuming him
[her dog Bounce] in "my old red plaid shawl,
and then I tied a handkerchief on his head and tied
an old veil anon and then we played organ grinder."

— KATHERINE C. GRIER, *Pets in America,*
quoting a diary entry by Emily Marshall Eliot

"Mom!" The wail is as plaintive as any sound in the universe. Yet it brings a smile to our faces every morning when we hear it. Our little black-and-white tuxedo cat, Cuddles, has perfected this plea for attention. When we have not served her breakfast, the situation elicits her call for mom. She knows how to get what she needs.

In addition to Cuddles, our animal family currently consists of our tabby, Speedy; our cocker spaniel, Leaf; and our cockatiel, Sunshine. They are our animal children, but they parent us as well. As their human mom and dad, we feed, care for, play with, show affection to, and exercise them. They reciprocate by being animal parents who make us smile, relieve our stress, comfort us, groom our hair (the bird), lick our fingers and faces (the dog and cats), and connect us to nature.

Our pets were our coparents when our children were little. Ours was an unusually blended family. Before we were married, Linda had adopted from Korea our son and daughter at the ages of five and seven, respectively. They arrived in the United States escorted by a volunteer Delta flight attendant who used her flying privileges to transport the children from an orphanage. They showed up at the airport with little bags of peanuts clutched in their hands, looking shell-shocked and not speaking one word of English.

One of their first experiences was meeting Linda's dog Lotus, a little Lhasa apso, and our curmudgeon of a cat, Mugsie, who eventually lived to the age of twenty-one — a benchmark for cats. Our daughter, Susan, recalls, "I had never been around dogs in Korea but I knew cats. The dog scared me. Mugsie made me feel comfortable in a place where every sight, sound, and smell was different from anything I had ever known. He used to rub his head against my leg to show me that he was there. Mugsie slept in my bed with me. At one of the loneliest and scariest times of my life, he made me know that I was never alone."

Later, we got married; Allen adopted the children, and as a family we adopted a beautiful golden retriever named Prana. She became a loving playmate for our son and daughter, greeting them happily when they came home from school. One of our sweetest memories is of watching our son throw sticks and balls for Prana in the backyard. She never tired of returning them. Her gentle nature served as a backdrop to every family scene and circumstance. As Susan says, "Prana was just always there."

Always There

In the stories told in *Animals and the Kids Who Love Them*, children and their parents are faced with what appear to be insurmountable obstacles to success. Animals have come into their lives and motivated them and given them the assistance they need to become so much more than anyone could have hoped for or expected. You're about to meet animals living in homes with children who face challenges most of us cannot imagine living with on a daily basis. Some of the stories in this book introduce children who readily experience sensory overload; touch is uncomfortable for them, even painful; they do not speak or cannot see or cannot walk. Shattered children, they have been blessed with pets who act as their Rosetta stone, helping them decipher the confusing world around them.

Other extraordinary stories in this book introduce animals who are not children's pets but who serve as their beacons of hope, healing, and compassion. Perhaps the moment of empathy occurs when a dog or cat visits a child's hospital room or after-school program. Maybe the animal is a guinea pig who curls up in a tiny basket and listens to a child read. A llama, turkey, chicken, goat, or horse draws children out of darkness and silence into the light and sound. A Dalmatian named Sparkles teaches them how to take care of themselves in case of a house fire. A golden retriever named Ricochet raises money to help kids with debilitating conditions. Whatever acts of kindness the animals perform for children, whom they may have met only once, have changed the kids' lives forever.

And then there are the stories in this book of pure childhood bliss with loyal pet playmates. A dog, cat, or rabbit patiently allows sticky hands to tug on his or her fur and gamely goes along with being fussed over or dressed up in necklaces and earrings. A dog protects a child, exhibiting loyalty and constancy that may never be equaled in adult life. A turtle entices a little boy to eat lettuce. These are the animals who befriend lonely children and spend quality time with boys or girls whose parents are burdened with life's innumerable responsibilities. They are Peter Pan, never growing up yet remembered even after the kids have forgotten other childhood treasures.

A Pet for Every Child?

In *Animals and the Kids Who Love Them*, animals befriend children just as they do in millions of the 62 percent of American households that have a pet.[1] Because of the documented close link between kids and pets, we interviewed Sonia C. Velazquez, former senior vice president of the American Humane Association. Her team provides research, training, and policies for child protection and advocacy and equips child protection agencies across the country with resources and information to help children, families, and communities thrive.

The American Humane Association, a national organization, has historical roots in protecting animals and children. Since its founding in 1877 by several humane organizations from across the United States, the American Humane Association has based a lot of its work on how the lives of animals and children are connected. The organization emphasizes that the word *humane* is not only for animals but also pertains to the well-being of all living creatures.

We asked Sonia to talk to us about the link between the welfare of animals and that of children. She explained that most families in the United States consider companion animals to be family members. "The well-being of children and animals in a family is inseparable. When animal maltreatment is happening in a home, other forms of maltreatment may also be occurring, and the family may be struggling."

Sonia's comments, and other interviews we did with contributing authors, led us to wonder if every home with children should have a pet. Is it possible for anything to make a child's life better or more fun than an animal companion in whom to confide secrets? A pet's warm presence can even cause a child to be less likely to suffer from asthma and to miss fewer days of school because of illness.[2]

We concluded, of course, that no matter how wonderful it might be to bring an animal into a family, pets are not right for everyone. There are important factors to consider before making the decision. After reading about the benefits that children, their families, and the animals in the stories presented here have gained by forming relationships with each other, our readers' next impulse might be to rush out and bring home a pet. We encourage you to read the interview in the back of this book in which Sonia makes many valuable comments, including suggestions and recommendations to help you decide if adopting a pet is best for your family and the animal.

Benefits of the Animal-Kid Connection

Not only can pets provide an emotional touchstone for children, they can also, in most homes, present a vital way of experiencing nature. Gail F. Melson writes in *Why the Wild Things Are*, "Pets have become the only nonhumans that continue to share children's daily lives.... For children and adults alike, pets stand in for all the members of the animal kingdom, permitting a distant, ritualized contact with other species."[3]

And when a family is in crisis, a pet can give a child comfort and reassurance. A study by Tanja Hoff and Reinhold Bergler of the Institute of Psychology at the University of Bonn in Germany found that, when six-to-eleven-year-old children were going through their parents' divorce, if there was a dog in the home the children showed significantly less aggressive behavior toward themselves and others. The dog served as a loving distraction, understanding friend, and listening partner. When parents quarreled, the dog provided a retreat from conflict for the child.[4]

And let's not forget the amazing potential for building a sense of responsibility by having children learn to care for a family pet. Caring for a pet builds character, and children grow into nurturing and compassionate adults who know how to keep commitments.

Having pets in the home can motivate children to consider a future spent helping animals in some way. Many people have told us about childhood pets who gave them so much unconditional love that, as adults, they were inspired to build careers in veterinary medicine or to become staff or volunteers at animal welfare and rescue organizations.

Over the years, we have also spoken with children and teenagers who love animals and want to volunteer at animal shelters. Typically they are turned away by shelters that don't want to assume responsibility if a child is injured while caring for animals at the shelter. But young people can raise funds for shelters, participate in publicity campaigns, and learn leadership skills by supporting animal rescue in ways that don't require them to work directly with animals.

Animal-Assisted Therapy

Several of this book's stories involve the fascinating practice of animal-assisted therapy (AAT). In a home with a valued pet, cultivating the interactions of a child and an animal happens naturally. But not all children have access to pets, or if they do, the interactions are not designed to permit therapeutic or educational benefits to occur. That's where AAT comes in. With the help of adults who are trained to facilitate the therapeutic interactions, AAT can serve as a catalyst for healing.

AAT may sound like something new, but it's been around a long time. In the ninth century, animals were included in therapy for people with disabilities in a program at a farm in Gheel, Belgium. And in 1792, Quakers established the York Retreat in England, where they incorporated caring for birds and rabbits into a therapy program for patients with mental illness. In the mid-nineteenth century, Florence Nightingale, an English nurse, was one of that country's first advocates of AAT for the restoration of health. In 1867, a German hospital began encouraging patients with epilepsy to interact with birds, cats, and horses.[5]

Perhaps one of the most influential proponents of early AAT was the American child-psychiatrist Boris Levinson. He discovered that a nonverbal child spoke to Levinson's dog prior to a therapy session, providing an opportunity for the therapist to communicate with the boy. Levinson is credited with coining the term *pet therapy* in 1964, and he is considered to be the creator of what eventually grew into modern-day AAT.[6]

Now, therapists can learn how to work with animals and hear about a child's history as he or she talks to a furry friend. Counselors can watch a child's way of relating to animals for signs of imbalance, anger, or aggression. Occupational therapists, like the wonderful Mona Sams in this book, can increase a child's coordination as he or she strokes a duck or puts a harness on a llama.

A nonprofit organization called Our Farm set out to evaluate the effectiveness of its education program, which employs AAT, by using a method based on the skill-card process described in *The Centaur's Lessons: The Companionable Zoo Method of Therapeutic Education Based Upon Contact with Animals and Nature Study*, by Aaron H. Katcher and Gregory G. Wilkins.[7] Our Farm's study of sixty-five children, which incorporated an experimental and a control group, concluded that animal-assisted therapy and education (AATE) "has large and broadly distributed therapeutic effects on children and adolescents with significant emotional and behavioral disturbances. Positive effects include decreases in undercontrolled and aggressive behavior. There were also positive effects in terms of improving client cooperation with instructors, the extent of engagement with learning, and the appropriateness of behavioral control in regular school classes." One of the most intriguing and hopeful outcomes of Our Farm's study was that the behavior of child clients who received AATE remained modified in a beneficial way after the clinical trial

was over. In other words, the benefits did not occur only at the time
the children interacted with animals, but were lasting.[8]

In *Animals and the Kids Who Love Them*, Diana Richett, an
American Humane Association volunteer, recounts some of her
poignant experiences with her disabled cat, Simon, who partners
with her to tutor inner-city children at a Denver housing project.
Delta Society, Therapy Dogs International, North American Riding for the Handicapped Association, and many other national and
local nonprofit groups offer training in, and services incorporating,
AAT. Michele A. Woellner of Blandon, Pennsylvania, wrote to us
about the kind of miraculous benefits that can occur through AAT.

> I once worked in a classroom with a young boy named
> Sean. His doctors told his parents that he would never be
> able to speak. The doctors were wrong. They were blind to
> the miracle of animal-assisted therapy.
>
> After much prayer and research, Sean's parents decided
> to try therapeutic horseback riding. Sean made an immedi-
> ate spiritual connection to a horse named Ali. He loved that
> horse so much; Ali touched Sean's soul and deepest emotions.
>
> Not long after beginning therapeutic horseback riding,
> Sean made his first sound. It was the sound of Ali's hooves
> as they touched the ground. As more time passed, Sean
> spoke his first word — Ali. With additional speech therapy,
> Sean continued to learn new words. Sean and Ali are living
> proof of the kind of miracle that can happen when a child
> and an animal connect with one another.[9]

And of course, the amazing work that service animals do for children and adults with epilepsy, diabetes, autism, blindness, deafness,
mobility impairments, and other conditions is well documented.
Service animals bring disabled children, who are typically isolated

and ignored, into the world. A child with a cute service dog becomes a magnet for peer interaction and conversation.

Humane Education

Parents have long grappled with children who are still in the process of learning how to relate positively to another being, by letting them interact with an animal in the home. But this isn't only a modern-day solution to the need for teaching healthy behavior. In *Pets in America*, Katherine C. Grier quotes *Letters to Mothers*, a book written by Lydia H. Sigourney for nineteenth-century moms: "If it [the infant] seizes a kitten by the back, or pulls its hair, show immediately by your own example, how it may be held properly, and soothed into confidence. Draw back the little hand, lifted to strike the dog. Perhaps it may not understand that it thus inflicts pain. But be strenuous in confirming an opposite habit."[10]

Fortunately today, parents and educators have a lot of help in teaching children to be kind to animals. The American Humane Association, the Humane Society of the United States, the American Society for the Prevention of Cruelty to Animals, People for the Ethical Treatment of Animals, the Latham Foundation, and the Pet Care Trust all have excellent materials and classroom curricula that will help make humane education programs successful. Public schools, parents, grandparents, children's museums, pet supply stores, animal shelters, and shopping malls can avail themselves of this material and teach kids how to treat animals with respect at home and in the natural environment.

How This Book Is Organized

There are many theories about why animals are so incredibly good at bringing out the best in children and adults — neoteny, biophilia, animal halo effect, oxytocin — look them up, if you wish. Rather than outline the theories textbook-style, we have chosen to present you with true-life, heartwarming, instructive stories that demonstrate the beauty and practicality of fostering child-animal connections. The names of many of the children involved in these stories have been changed, and in some cases their identities have been obscured further, although the rest of the details are factual. The first time a fictitious name is used for a child, it is enclosed within quotation marks to alert readers to the change. Occasionally, the child depicted in the narrative is different from the one shown in the photo accompanying it. This is to protect children whose privacy needs to be preserved.

We encourage you to read the contributing authors' brief biographies at the back of this book. Many of them include website contact information for the authors and for organizations they mention in their stories. These nonprofits do amazing work for children and need your donations, volunteer help, and support.

You also may appreciate using the meditations at the end of each story. They are questions we pose for those readers who want to take a moment to reflect on their own childhoods and experiences with animals.

Now we invite you to join us as we enter into the world of children and animals. It is a world that thrills with its wonder, comfort, imagination, and adventures of the heart. Some of the cutest kids and animals on the planet are snuggled up together within these pages.

PART ONE

··

Hope

The mouse asks the beloved frog,
Do you know
what you are to me? During the day,
you're my energy for working. At night,
you're my deepest sleep.

— JALAL AL-DIN RUMI (1207–1273), "The Long String"

Miniature Horse Patty Pat Answers a Parent's Prayer

Tom Russo, WEST COXSACKIE, NEW YORK,
as told to Peggy Frezon, RENSSELAER, NEW YORK

Most kids get the sniffles, a cough, or a sore throat now and then. But my daughter, Tory, gets sick a lot. A common cold can send her to the hospital. Or worse, can lead to serious complications. Tory has common variable immunodeficiency. It's an immune disease similar to that of "the boy in the plastic bubble," who had to live in protective surroundings because his immune system couldn't keep him safe from germs. Fortunately, we don't have to keep Tory in a bubble. Our doctor encourages us to take her outdoors, let her spend time with other kids when she can, and lead as normal a life as possible.

When Tory was five, she had bronchitis ten times in as many months, and each time we rushed her off to the doctor for antibiotics or to the hospital for intravenous infusions of medication. One time as we drove home, my mind was clouded with worry. I glanced in the rearview mirror at my daughter, terribly thin, her fine blonde hair sticking to her pale cheeks, and thought, God, why does my child have this horrible disease? But then I heard soft sounds from the back seat. Tory was singing cheerfully. If she could bear it, I could be strong, too.

Several days later, Tory was feeling much better. "Let's take her to Newkirk's," I suggested to my wife, Lisa. My friend Newkirk owned King Hill Miniatures, a horse farm in Freehold, New York, Tory's favorite place to visit. A day in the country would do her good.

She loved the miniature horses and knew most of them by name, including a rebellious young horse, Patty, who was her favorite.

Tory was the first one in the car. She wore her brown cowboy boots that reached nearly to her knees, and her favorite shirt with the pony designs. As we drove alongside the pastures of King Hill Miniatures, I watched the little horses kick up their heels in the warm sunshine. Full of spring friskiness, they galloped and cavorted. Tory clapped her hands and, when the car stopped, opened the door and dashed out to the pasture gate.

Newkirk was there to meet us. "Watch out for Patty. She's a ramrod today," he cautioned us. He'd had his hands full with the young, silver chestnut mare from the day he got her. "I can't do anything with that horse," he'd complain. "She never listens to me, raises Cain on the farm, and runs around like a demon!"

Tory squeezed through the gate. Unfortunately, she had one thing on her mind. "Patty!" she called, clapping loudly.

Lisa caught up with her and grasped Tory's hand. "Let's go see the other horses."

But Tory shook her head firmly. "Patty Pat!" she called.

In the distance, Patty raised her head from the grass. When Tory called again, the horse perked up her ears and turned toward her and Lisa. Then she bolted their way like a streak of lightning. No one had time to stop her. Lisa threw her arms around Tory as the horse bore down on them. I charged toward them, and Newkirk ran to catch the horse. Tory, however, relaxed in Lisa's embrace, her little arm stretched out, reaching for the horse.

When Patty was only a breath away, something amazing happened. Instead of ramming into us or bucking or displaying any of the other wild behavior Newkirk had told us about, Patty stopped dead in her tracks. She whinnied softly, like she was saying "hello." Her deep brown eyes stared directly at Tory. Something in the horse's expression told me she sensed she should be gentle with this child. Tory reached up and touched Patty's silky neck.

Newkirk stared, his eyes wide, his mouth hanging open. "That horse never does that for me," he said. "When I call her, she runs the other way like a rocket!"

Patty lowered her nose and sniffed Tory, who giggled. Lisa loosened her grip on our daughter as Tory reached out and hugged the horse. Patty stood still and let Tory walk all around her, kissing her. Lisa wiped a tear from her eye, and I admit that I got choked up too, seeing how tender this horse became with our daughter. The two wandered around the field together, the miniature horse and the little girl, fast friends, until it was time to go. Then Patty followed Tory to the gate.

"I don't get it," said Newkirk, shaking his head. "She's never done that before. For anyone. You've seen her, wild as the day she was born."

As our car pulled away, Tory twisted around in her seat, trying to see Patty. And what was Patty doing? Pawing at the pasture gate as if she wanted to follow us home.

Tory's New Best Friend

From then on, we brought Tory to the farm to visit Patty as often as we could. Newkirk even let us buy Patty and keep her at his place. Patty was just as wild as ever, except when Tory was around, and then she turned calm and docile. No one could explain it.

Tory's effect on Patty was clear. But just as amazing was Patty's effect on Tory. When Tory started school, she missed so many days due to illness that we eventually had to have her home-tutored. She couldn't play contact sports or join in other active games with kids her age. Going outside our home was awkward; sometimes she had to wear a mask to protect her from germs. Lisa and I worried about her missing out on a social life, which is so important to young girls. Few mothers felt comfortable including Tory on sleepovers;

they didn't want the responsibility of dealing with an emergency brought on by her medical issues.

Every time our daughter got sick, a scary thought lurked in the back of my mind. What if this time she didn't respond to the treatments? What if she didn't get better? Tory didn't have a life like other little girls: every two weeks she endured intravenous infusions of immune globulins. The side effects left her sick and exhausted for days. It crushed me to see her like that. When Tory curled up in a ball on the couch, quiet and motionless, I worried — what if she loses the will to go on?

At night, I could hear Lisa sobbing into her pillow. Her whispered prayer was, "God, I know she is your child, and you know what's best. But my daughter is so weak. Sometimes we feel helpless." I would add my own silent prayer. I tried to be strong, even though at times I felt helpless too.

But when Tory saw Patty, everything was different. We'd pull up the drive to the farm, and she'd jump out of the car, head toward the pasture, and call, "Where's my Patty Pat?" Every time, the horse came galloping to her.

When Tory felt well, she and Patty ran together in the field. When she didn't feel well, Tory sat on the ground, and Patty stood over her like a sentry. One time when Tory was too weak to play outside, I pulled up a chair and sat her in front of the stall, and Patty pushed her nose over the door. I left them together for a while so I could talk with Newkirk. When I returned, Tory's schoolbooks lay open on her lap, and she was

Tory and Patty

reading aloud to Patty. "Dad, she's going to be the smartest horse in the world," Tory told me, beaming. I laughed and hugged my daughter tightly.

How They Heal and Comfort Each Other

One day Patty suffered a devastating injury. She cut the tendon sheath on the back of her leg. She allowed no one to change her bandages. "She hates people messing with her legs," Newkirk said.

The horse had been thrashing and kicking with her nostrils flaring and eyes bulging. But when we brought Tory to the stable, Patty's eyes softened. With her gaze glued to Tory, she let us change her bandages, standing stalk still as Tory talked and sang to her.

Tory still struggles with her illness, but whenever she gets down, she thinks about Patty and smiles. Illness after illness, treatment after treatment, somehow she gets through, and the first thing she wants to do is to see Patty. It's even easier now because Patty came to live with us. Tory can watch her best friend right from her bedroom window. There's no way we can know why Patty is calm only for Tory. Or how Tory draws strength and hope from the little horse. I just know that Patty is in our little girl's life for a reason.

"Where's my Patty Pat?" calls Tory. And I know the answer. She's by your side and in your heart, the answer to a parent's prayers. For hope comes in many forms, even in the shape of a rebellious little horse.

Meditation

What are the ways animals or other people have answered your prayers and given you hope? How could you pass on to others the gift of hope?

Midas Makes Our Dream Come True

Julie Yanz, MINNEAPOLIS, MINNESOTA

My son Zach began his life meeting every developmental milestone along the way. He was a charming, happy little boy who loved to kick a ball around the backyard, scribble at the kitchen table, and nestle in my lap for a good squeeze. He would point at planes flying overhead and use words to describe what he saw in the world.

When Zach was fourteen months old, his demeanor changed drastically. Within a couple of months his emerging language gave way to grunts and screams. Crying, he erupted into fits of rage and self-injury. His fine and gross motor skills were gone. He couldn't kick a ball or hold a crayon in his little hands. He did not want clothes on his body. The slightest touch on his skin could prompt a fight-or-flight response. He was up for hours on end, never sleeping except when I held him against my chest. He no longer smiled, and the sparkle in his eyes was gone. It was as if a candlesnuffer had lowered on him and extinguished his light. The child I had known vanished into the dark cave of regressive autism.

I remember leaning over Zach's bed as he finally fell asleep one night and begging for his once-emerging language to return and explode into sentences. I pleaded for his body to move and respond the way it had.

We frantically began the race of our lives to get our son back. Almost immediately we began intensive, thirty-five-hour-a-week therapy in our home. In addition I shuttled Zach to speech and occupational therapy several times a week. Often his siblings and I would cheer him on through the smoked glass in the observation room as he relearned how to toss a ball. We rejoiced in the small victories he made over autism, such as learning how to blow so he could blow out the candles on his birthday cake. We incorporated music and aquatic therapy, special diets and supplements, and countless doctor appointments — all in an effort to regain our son.

As I look back on those early years, it was clear Zach made gains. He did relearn some of what autism took from him. But our family struggled and found it challenging to function anymore as a unit. Most days we had caregivers or therapists in our home, and Zach became accustomed to one-on-one therapy. I found it difficult to balance his needs with my need to have my family together — alone. Truth was, it was hard to do anything outside of the home unless we had help.

I could not control the variables of daily life to make Zach more successful in his efforts to progress. Everyday noises such as lawnmowers, motorcycles, the drumming of an overhead light fixture, and the vacuum were disturbing to him. His senses were always in a state of high alert, and his behavior was unpredictable. The older he got, the harder it was for him to control his flailing arms and legs. His fists would pummel his head until it was swollen and black and blue. He would bite and break his skin, becoming even more aggressive after he saw the blood he had drawn.

When we went outside our home, I couldn't take my eyes off Zach or he'd be gone — maybe not quickly, but quietly for sure. If he did run away, I couldn't always catch him. A few times, he darted in front of cars.

I had to do something. Our house was safe. Our backyard was safe. But our life was not safe. Our family found solace at home and could relax there, but the isolation hurt us all. My heart ached as I tried to figure out another way we could live as a family, with autism. This was no longer a sprint but a marathon. We continued to hope that Zach would be one of those children who broke through the locks of autism.

Golden Midas

In the summer of 2008 I saw an interview on television regarding Can Do Canines' autism assistance dogs. It sparked my hope that one day Zach could have an assistance dog, and I applied for one right away. When I read the organization's mission statement, I knew we had found the right group: "Can Do Canines is dedicated to enhancing the quality of life for people with disabilities by creating mutually beneficial partnerships with specially trained dogs. We envision a world where everyone who wants and needs an assistance dog can have one."

This mission and dream resonated with me. I was thrilled to envision my child living life to his own potential with the help of a special dog. Years of focusing on cognitive skills and behavioral strategies had left Zach without social skills. It was time to change that. The next leg of the marathon would be to focus on socialization by engaging my son with his family and with life in the world beyond our home. I believed that an autism assistance dog would be the perfect companion for Zach on this journey. After we submitted an application and participated in interviews and a home visit, Zach was accepted as a candidate for an autism assistance dog.

In January 2010, after a two-year wait, Zach visited with a gorgeous, eighty-pound golden retriever named Midas, and we had our first glimpse of what was to come. While Midas was not yet fully trained, it was as though he instantly knew Zach was the boy he was learning to help. The dog approached my son with a gentle enthusiasm that prompted Zach to reach out and touch the large head nestled in his lap. It was clear that Zach had found a friend in Midas. After several months of training with Can Do Canines, Midas came home to live with Zach on May 5, 2010. Every day since then, we have appreciated the many ways Midas enhances our lives and encourages Zach to live life to the fullest.

Midas does what traditional service dogs do; but to a child with autism, he also gives a myriad of other meaningful gifts countless times every day. He offers a soft landing spot for Zach's toes and lets Zach's fingers twirl his fur on a long car ride. His scratchy tongue licks Zach's face and hands when our son is frustrated, eventually turning tears into a smile. He cozies up and rubs his smooth ears against Zach's cheek as reassurance that he is there for him. All these small gestures offer Zach a friendship that no one else can provide. No words are spoken. No words are needed. Their communication is clear to those who witness it — this is the unconditional love between a boy and his dog.

Zach's world is expanding with Midas by his side. As a constant companion, Midas is Zach's anchor, both physically and emotionally.

When they are in public together, Midas is at times a literal physical anchor. He and Zach are tethered together by a six-foot lead that connects a belt around Zach's waist to a harness worn by Midas. I hold on to a leash connected to Midas. If Zach bolts away suddenly, Midas is trained to firmly stand in one place and hold his ground, not allowing Zach to run away no matter how hard he pulls. This keeps Zach safe and allows me to relax more.

Midas acts as Zach's emotional anchor when his presence calms Zach during anxious times of overstimulation. Midas makes it possible for Zach to participate in things we hadn't previously been able to do as a family.

Most families take for granted the idea of eating dinner out together. Before Midas, Zach wouldn't sit still for a meal. One parent would have to stay with the other kids while the other parent took Zach out of the restaurant before he had a tantrum. This summer,

we went on a family vacation with Midas and Zach. The highlight of one weekend was an evening when our family of five sat

Zach and Midas

in a restaurant and enjoyed
dinner. Zach's siblings were
overjoyed that we were actually all together, and Zach
was content. He was able to
take off his shoes and rest
his feet on his friend's back.
Physical connection through
the tether kept Zach feeling grounded. If he got up
from his chair, he couldn't
walk very far. Midas kept him
within arm's reach, and Zach
would quickly sit back down.

I am certain Zach even tossed a few fries under the table to keep
Midas happy.

Another highlight was attending Christmas Eve Mass as a
family. Before Midas came to us, Zach was not able to tolerate the
crowds and noises that are part of an event like that. He would
become overwhelmed and want to run or have a tantrum. In fact,
Midas was a key figure in improving the behavior of all the kids
in the congregation — they were fascinated to see a dog at church.
Midas made the experience positive by staying at Zach's side, taking
walking breaks in the hall with him or snuggling to let Zach pet his
furry coat.

Midas's greatest gift is the way he allows us to find enjoyment in
being together and doing things like other families. Activities such
as going to the pool, the park, or on a walk used to be very short
in duration. Now we can stay longer because Zach calms himself
with Midas's help. Midas and Zach attend my daughter's volleyball

games, swim meets, and science fairs. We go to Zach's brother's baseball games and hockey tournaments. It is Zach's turn to cheer on his siblings.

I can turn my back when we are out in public and know that Zach is still nearby. I observe an increased sense of independence in him. By having a job to do — holding on to Midas's harness — Zach gets the chance to be responsible. By forming a partnership with my son, Midas allows Zach to venture where there are other people. Zach no longer has to cope with social situations alone; Midas is there to give him comfort when he feels stressed.

Midas is Zach's built-in sensory regulator. His calm demeanor and fluffy body are just what my son needs to tolerate life. Autism is still present for Zach and our family, but it no longer defines us. Midas has helped us find the balance we were searching for.

Zach feels connected to Midas when dealing with difficult or disturbing situations. Midas takes the pressure off Zach, since, by being a cute dog, he attracts most of the attention. Midas is also a visual sign to others that Zach needs additional help. People are more understanding and compassionate when they see my son with his service dog. Midas's presence helps Zach socialize more, because people always want to ask questions or pet the dog. And as I have learned, Midas, like all golden retrievers, loves the attention.

Midas's spirit has encouraged my son to be comfortable and more self-confident. With his unconditional love, he has taught Zach to trust and rely on him. Their friendship has blossomed into so much more than we ever imagined. There are moments every single day that we are grateful for the role Midas plays in Zach's life, and for how he has changed our family.

Our journey with Midas and Zach has helped us to accept our reality — Zach has autism, but he is still a delightful, loving, non-conversational child with a sparkle in his eye and a desire to live life. We changed our course of treating and managing autism. It is *part* of Zach's life; it doesn't *rule* his life. We dreamed that Zach would break through the locks of autism. With the help of a wonderful and loving dog, the dream has come true.

Meditation

When there has been calamity or even despair in your life, has an animal come along who gave you hope for the future? Can you pass that hope along to others with your own actions?

Surf Dog Ricochet
Changes the World for Children

....

Judy Fridono, SAN DIEGO, CALIFORNIA

Q: How does a puppy who was intended to be a service dog go from failing at that plan to raising more than seventy thousand dollars for children with disabilities and other charitable causes while becoming a national-award-winning star of a video clip viewed more than 3 million times on YouTube?

A: By doing what she loves — surfing.

Because my golden retriever–Lab mix, Rina, helps me to conserve my energy, retrieves objects, picks up mail, and does other tasks that make daily life easier, I know the value of a service dog for someone like me with chronic pain or a disability. That is why I was drawn to work, through my nonprofit organization Puppy Prodigies, with prospective service dogs, as puppies, to stimulate their brain development. At the time I began this work, I didn't know it would positively affect the lives of children with special needs and bring a dog I love into the international spotlight.

At birth, puppies have only the senses of smell and touch. As part of my job, I introduce puppies to many different scents and have them feel fabrics, such as satin and burlap, against their skin. After the puppies open their eyes and ears, I enhance their brain functioning with a variety of sounds and sights. Then I work on their balance and coordination by having them walk in a whelping box or crawl up and around objects on uneven surfaces. I make the tasks more challenging and fun as they continue to grow. When they are eight weeks old, I send the puppies to Paws'itive Teams and other service dog organizations, where they will continue their training.

Out of a litter of golden retriever puppies born in my home on January 25, 2008, only three were female. An ultrasound had been done on the mom a few weeks earlier, and it had shown that she carried ten puppies. I wanted to keep a girl puppy, because they often have the specific temperament to become service dogs. So the more girls to choose from in the litter, the better the odds that I would find one to train.

After the first two females were born, I said out loud, "Make the next puppy a girl with a little patch of white fur on her chest." That request came from nowhere, and I didn't know why I was saying the words. The next puppy born was a female with a white patch of fur on her chest. I kept her and planned to name her Que Sera Sera (What Will Be Will Be) because I wasn't sure which service dog program she would enter by the time she turned two years old.

I started behavior training with the puppy when she was thirteen days old. She learned to climb on some things, follow a food source, and walk in circles. At six weeks of age, the active girl literally bounced off walls, so I named her Ricochet. I think we are all on a spiritual journey, and nothing happens by coincidence — the name *Ricochet* would reflect the turnabout her life, and mine, was about to take. By the time she was eight weeks old, I had taught her such service dog requirements as dragging a laundry basket, getting Kleenex when I sneezed, and turning on lights. I had also started to work on her balance and coordination, which would be enhanced by teaching her to surf.

Losing Ricochet's Interest

Ricochet continued doing very well with my training. In fact, I'd call her a brilliant puppy — amazingly smart, willing to learn, and easy to train and motivate with food. But at about fourteen to six-teen weeks, she lost interest in training, sports, and every other activity we were doing together. I knew her potential, but she wasn't giving it to me anymore. I tried to figure out what was wrong. Why had she stopped performing at the level I knew she could reach?

At about nine months, she developed an interest in chasing things, especially birds, so we worked on self-control. It would be dangerous for her, as a service dog, to give in to her chase instinct. Even though she was ultimately able to control it, there was no guarantee she wouldn't take off after a bird, and this was problem-atic. A service dog can't give in to the chase instinct even once while attached to a person's wheelchair.

When she was about sixteen weeks to fourteen months old, Ricochet and I struggled with each other. I wanted her to be what I intended, and she was not living up to my expectations. Reluctantly I tried to accept that, because of her interest in running after birds, she could not qualify as a service dog. Still, I held on to the hope that she would improve.

In June 2009, Ricochet was invited to the Purina Incredible Dog Challenge, where top dogs compete in different sports such as catching Frisbees (or flying discs), negotiating obstacles in a timed dog-agility competition, jumping, and surfing, in which dogs ride surfboards by themselves with humans pushing the boards into the waves. Even though Ricochet had practiced in a bay and a swim-ming pool, she had been in the ocean for the first time only two weeks before the contests. Yet she won third place in the surfing challenge. I got the thrill of seeing that she could accomplish some-thing and be good at it.

During the month after her surfing win, I observed that Rico-chet could control her impulses and be trained. But I knew that I couldn't guarantee she wouldn't chase inappropriately. So in July

2009, when she was fifteen months old, I conceded that Ricochet would be my family pet instead of a service dog.

An Idea Is Born

I went to a couple of surf dog contests in San Diego to take some pictures. As I watched the dogs, I thought about Ricochet's great balance and coordination. She had such good balance that she could crawl into a hammock while it was rocking back and forth, and stand there. I realized I could continue teaching her to surf by working with her on a boogie board in the swimming pool at home. I thought maybe she could enter a surfing contest for fun when we spent time at the beach.

The day after I made my decision to release her from the service dog role, Ricochet lay under my desk while I wondered what this dog's purpose in life might be. What could she do that would be meaningful? Then it occurred to me that surfing might be her way of serving.

As I sat at my computer with these thoughts tumbling through my mind, it felt like energy and creativity were channeling through me. Before I knew it, I had designed a website and a new concept that involved Ricochet surfing to raise funds for people with disabilities. If she couldn't be a service dog herself, maybe she could help people get the money they needed in order to have service dogs.

An overwhelmingly positive feeling that I had never experienced flowed through me. Until then, I had been a pretty negative person as a result of living with the pain of my own disabilities, which include rheumatoid arthritis, chronic fatigue, fibromyalgia, chronic pain, and other autoimmune disorders. At last I knew what it was like to feel joyous and powerful. The floodgates opened, and

I released Ricochet. Looking down at her by my feet, I said, "Okay, be who you are."

Ricochet and Patrick

After launching Ricochet on a new career path, I heard that Paws'itive Teams was getting ready to match one of their dogs with Patrick Ivison, a fifteen-year-old boy with disabilities. Patrick was an adaptive surfer, a term describing a person who uses a surfboard adapted to his or her disability. In September 1995, when Patrick was fourteen months old, he and his mother were walking behind a parked car as an uninsured, distracted driver backed up suddenly and ran over him, pinning him under the car. He suffered an incomplete spinal cord injury — of his fourth and fifth cervical vertebrae — and became quadriplegic.

Patrick doesn't remember the accident, but he has used a wheelchair ever since. Still, he is an active boy who focuses on what he can do, not on what he can't do. Today, Patrick enjoys surfing, playing hockey, rugby, basketball, and snow skiing. But when I met him, a few days after I released Ricochet from her service dog work, Patrick's life was quite different, as he and his mother, Jennifer Kayler, dealt with the aftereffects and expenses of his accident.

When he was ten, Patrick started going to Project Walk for intensive physical therapy. There, he built strength by exercising parts of his body he couldn't move or control. His muscles had shortened and tightened; his posture had deteriorated. Project Walk's therapy program elongated his muscles, increased his strength, and improved his posture. His range of motion in his arms and legs increased, and Patrick gained movement in his hands, allowing him to pick up items. Before long, he was able to do things he had thought impossible.

But treatments at Project Walk cost one hundred dollars per

hour, and Patrick required six hours of treatment per week for at least three years. His family needed money in order for him to continue. His dream was to walk across the stage for his high school graduation in 2012, and he longed to one day live an independent life and attend college.

Paws'itive Teams staff saw a video of Ricochet on a surfboard and asked me to send Patrick a video of her surfing. They thought he would get a kick out of seeing my dog ride the waves. Patrick and I emailed back and forth a couple of times, and I soon learned about his need for someone to raise funds.

Patrick was a surfer with disabilities and a dream. Ricochet was a surfer dog I had dreamed would be a service dog. They sounded like a good match to me. Ricochet could raise funds to help Patrick continue his therapy. I called Jennifer and asked if they would be interested in a fund-raiser that involved Patrick and my dog surfing together. She told me that Patrick was excited at the prospect of surfing with Ricochet. We arranged for boy and dog to meet, and they immediately connected.

The next day, I made a video that captured Ricochet running up to Patrick on the beach. Patrick describes the experience by saying, "Ricochet took a flying leap into my lap and licked my face. I knew right away that I had never met a dog like her." She had been introduced to him the evening before and spent only a half hour with him, but they had forged an immediate bond. It was clear that she adored Patrick.

To promote the fund-raiser, I planned to have Patrick and Ricochet surf on their individual boards but on the same wave, side by side, and to videotape it. The day before the two of them were to surf, I sent a press release to the local San Diego media. Reporters and cameras from four television news stations showed up at the beach to meet us the next day.

To everyone's delight, the crews were able to film Patrick and Ricochet surfing next to each other on a few waves. My dog's energy was palpable. And then, something incredible happened when they reached shore. Ricochet jumped off her board and climbed onto Patrick's, as if she wanted to surf with him instead of only by his side.

I asked Patrick's surfing coach, "Do you want to give this a try?" He and Patrick were game. Patrick's coach went home quickly and found a bigger surfboard. When he returned to the beach, I said, "I'll position Ricochet on the board. I have to trust her. I can't tell her how to surf with Patrick. She just knows what to do, so let her do it." Patrick's instructor hon-ored my request. The team took Ricochet and Patrick out into knee-deep water. His lower body lay flat on the surfboard, and he lifted his upper body with his elbows so he could look straight ahead. With Ricochet at Patrick's back, we shoved their surfboard off on a wave.

There was barely room for Ricochet on the board, and she couldn't straddle Patrick. She had to take a stance different from the one she used when she surfed alone. Still, she managed to provide balance and strength

Ricochet and Patrick

with her body positioned behind Patrick's. I was amazed when Ricochet surfed as if they had been doing it together forever. Patrick describes the experience of surfing with her as "surreal."

They surfed all the way into the beach. I felt a little apprehen-sive, because when Ricochet was eight weeks old and in the early stages of learning the sport, she would surf for a while and then want to go play with other dogs. But with Patrick she kept running back into the water to surf again and again. She never said, "I'm done." To see her energy and watch her surf so successfully with Patrick made me believe she had been born again in the water. This is what she was here to do. She had found her purpose.

Knowing how much Ricochet enjoyed all the other times I had taken her out surfing, I understood that she wanted to play with Patrick. Everybody at the beach who was helping us that day felt the excitement and petted her and clapped. She was so happy. Whenever I had tried to train her to be a service dog, she had picked up on my frustration. But that day, she made me proud and knew I accepted her. It was a magical turning point for both of us.

After that day, Ricochet and I continued to raise money to support Patrick's therapy by letting Ricochet and him surf together and donating the funds to his campaign, "Help Patrick Walk." We also did demonstrations at surf contests. Sometimes Ricochet moved in between his legs and bent one front paw over his butt. I didn't know how she counterbalanced the board and kept him from falling off it — how could she balance him when she was off-balance herself? It was amazing to watch.

On YouTube.com, I posted the video *From Service Dog to SURFice Dog* to show Patrick and Ricochet surfing in tandem and Ricochet balancing behind Patrick on the surfboard. It quickly went viral. To date, the video has been viewed more than 3 million times. Many people have written to tell me they've shown the video to students, teachers, life coaches, inmates at women's prisons, and anyone else who needs to see that it's possible to transform disappointment by heading in a joyful new direction. With the video's worldwide exposure, I was able to expand our new platform to include other ways of helping humans and animals. I called Ricochet's mission "Pawing It Forward" as a takeoff on the concept of "paying it forward."

Patrick says, "I surfed before meeting Ricochet, and that was cool. But who knew I needed to add a dog to the picture? What Ricochet has done is like a drop of water in a lake, and the ripples keep extending on and on." Jennifer adds, "We truly had no idea how life-changing that day on the beach was going to be. It is hard to put into words the incredible effect Ricochet and Judy have had on my son's life. Ricochet has given him the gift of recovery. It will continue to increase his independence and quality of life. Ricochet and Judy are like family to us. We've had so many experiences and made new friends as a result of our friendship with them."

Ricochet and Ian

Ricochet's next project was to raise funds for and awareness about a six-year-old brain-injured child, Ian McFarland. A friend emailed me Ian's story, drawn from newspaper and TV coverage. I called a contact I had at the TV station and asked to get in touch with the family. When I talked to Ian's aunt, Melissa Coleman, she explained that Ian had been in a car accident in July 2008 that had claimed the lives of his parents. The boy and his dad had been passionate about surfing, Melissa said. "Ian's first steps after the accident were in the ocean, and it is very healing to him. He loved surfing with his dad. But he was scared of it now."

I wanted to see if Ian would surf with Ricochet. Surfing with a six-year-old child who could be easily distracted would be different from surfing with Patrick. By this time, Ricochet was two years old and easily distracted too. Ian liked to build sandcastles. Ricochet liked to chase birds. I wondered if they would relate to each other. The two met at a park near Ian's house and played ball. Melissa described their first meeting like this: "There was an immediate bonding. Ian had a huge smile on his face and he laughed at Ricochet's every hug and kiss."

Ricochet and Ian

When they got together on the beach for the first time, Ricochet was able to bring joy back to Ian as they mounted a surfboard and rode the waves together. Ian was no longer afraid, and the two of them have surfed together many times since. Melissa says, "Ricochet makes Ian happy and confident. This carries over to his physical abilities. He continues the rehabilitation process and is growing stronger. Surfing has helped his core muscles and improved his sense of balance, which is one of the last steps in learning to walk again independently." Ricochet became Ian's playmate and friend. Whenever they are in the same area, Ricochet always finds Ian in the crowd and rushes over to greet him.

The money we raised for Ian helped him to have hippotherapy (therapeutic horseback riding), as well as physical, occupational, and aqua therapy. Ian's neurosurgeon says that the aggressive therapy has helped Ian get to where he is today, and that the boy needs it to continue his remarkable recovery. Melissa says, "We are so thankful and honored to have Ricochet and Judy in our lives. They have made a huge impact on Ian's recovery and, ultimately, changed his life forever."

On my website, I posted video clips of Ian and Ricochet surfing together, one of which includes footage from a camera Ricochet wore on her back. Ricochet's SURFice dog video, which attracts thousands of viewers a day, continues to raise funds for the child.

Ricochet Brings Joy to the World

Ian's and Patrick's media attention and viral videos have enabled Ricochet to help children in yet another way. We have now held two Surfin' Santa Paws toy drives for children and animals. The beneficiaries are Rady Children's Hospital, where we distribute toys Ricochet has helped to buy, and Helen Woodward Animal Center, where we donate toys for shelter animals. In 2010, Ricochet raised $9,070 for the Christmas toy drive. After the first toy drive ended, and while our videos were being viewed at their highest rate, I asked Ian's family if we could add a link to Ian's website and ask for donations to him too. The video and Ricochet's Facebook fans raised over $7,500 dollars for him.

I believe Ricochet understands her journey and knows exactly what she's here for. Early on, she showed me what she wanted to do. She has let me play a role as one of her facilitators. If I hadn't accepted what she showed me, I wouldn't have been successful in helping her achieve her mission.

The media have been extremely helpful in bringing Ricochet's story to the public. Ricochet's tale has been told by national media such as *USA Today* and the *Today* show, as well as by numerous pet and general interest magazines. After Ricochet asked for his help, San Diego Mayor Jerry Sanders proclaimed April 29, 2010, as Pay It Forward Day. With Ricochet by my side, I gave out dog biscuits to doggie commuters near a San Diego transit station where the ceremony was held.

To date, Ricochet has raised donations for causes such as the Association of Amputee Surfers, Wheels 2 Water, Ocean Healing Group, Chase Away K9 Cancer, and many more. In December 2010 the American Kennel Club honored her with one of its Awards for Canine Excellence for her commitment to helping others, and she received the award in a ceremony, broadcast later on national television, at the AKC/Eukanuba National Championship in January 2011. Out of hundreds of nominees for this award, each year only five dogs are honored for performing an exemplary act or series of acts that have benefited communities or individuals. Ricochet's name is engraved on a plaque permanently displayed at the AKC Library's Wall of Fame in New York City.

I'm hoping to inspire other people who suffer from chronic illness to realize that they can do much that is meaningful. It is a wonderful thing for me to have gone from being negative to doing something that gives me purpose. People say Ricochet changed them. One young girl mentioned that she had considered harming herself, but that, after seeing Ricochet's video, she didn't do it. Ricochet's service is no doubt more far-reaching than any of us know.

Meditation

Sometimes we are expected to take a certain course, but then the light shines on a different path. What has given you hope when you were faced with detours and a change of direction?

A Cat Therapist for David

Thuvan DeBellis, JACKSONVILLE, FLORIDA

Have you ever wanted something so badly, it was all you thought about? When my husband and I decided to have another baby, I wished and prayed for a boy. I was already blessed with two beautiful, gifted, and intelligent girls, Sarah, age ten, and Kathryn, age six. When my doctor called me at home to tell me my third child would be a boy, I felt ecstatic. Then he said my baby also had Down syndrome.

I sat at home on my couch, by myself, and cried. Why did I have to be the one out of two hundred women who would have a baby born with Down's? My friend told me God never gives us more than we can handle. At the time, I thought that was easy for her to say, because she was not the one having a baby with special needs.

As I forged through denial and entered the acceptance stage, a whirlwind of questions filled my head and occupied my days. Would my husband and I be good parents? Would we be ready when the time came? How severe would our child's disability be? How could my family cope with a baby who had special needs? Would we have to give away our family cat, Toby, a Maine coon we'd had for two years? We had heard horror stories about how some animals become aggressive toward a newborn baby, especially if the animal is very territorial or resents no longer being the center of attention.

27

We decided to name the baby David. He was born beautiful, with a head full of coal black hair, dark brown eyes, and slightly yellowish skin due to the jaundice that is very common in premature babies whose livers are not fully developed. The delivery nurses immediately put him on oxygen and placed him in an incubator in the neonatal intensive care unit. He remained under a bilirubin lamp for about two weeks to continue treating and curing his jaundice.

David was born with a congenital heart disease, which meant he had a hole in his heart that would eventually require open-heart surgery. Since he weighed only five pounds, his cardiologist suggested we wait until he was five months old before going ahead with the surgery. Unfortunately, after three months David began to show signs of heart failure. My husband and I drove to Shand's Children's Hospital at the University of Florida in Gainesville for our son's open-heart surgery.

The surgery was a success. Seeing David connected to tubes and wires scared me, but I knew we'd found the best facility to take care of him. I did not realize at the time that, often when babies like David have open-heart surgery, it is common for them to forget how to suck on a nipple. So teaching my three-month-old baby to feed again became imperative. When his energy level began to diminish, he received a blood transfusion, which raised his red blood cell count. Then at last we were allowed to bring him home.

During the few months that preceded David's birth, my husband and I had researched Down syndrome and learned how to get Toby ready for the new arrival. My husband took the blanket from David's hospital crib and wrapped David in it. Then he brought it home for Toby to sniff so that he would be accustomed to the baby's new scent.

When we brought David home from the hospital the first time, we carried him into the house and, while the baby was still in his car seat, set him on the floor for Toby to smell. Toby sniffed David while my husband sat on the floor and lifted the baby out of the car seat. He held David in his arms and petted Toby at the same time. All the preparation worked. To our relief Toby accepted David well. He did not exhibit any aggressive behaviors, such as hissing, scratching, or biting. He simply lay next to the baby and my husband and allowed himself to be petted and pampered.

After his surgery, David had to remain on his back for two months. While other five-month-old babies would be flipping onto their stomachs, grasping at objects, and cooing, David had to stare at the ceiling, allowing for little developmental growth. We encouraged his cognitive development by reading many books to him, and his sisters sang to him often. Toby continued to remain near David. A couple of times, we caught him jumping into David's crib when David was out of the room. Our crib was unusual in that instead of the whole side sliding down,

David and Toby

the top quarter of the railing folded down. Given the large size of a Maine coon cat, Toby could stand on his hind legs and stretch to reach the top of the crib's lowered railing with his paws.

Four months later, I arranged for David to receive physical therapy through Early Steps, Florida's special needs program. Diane, a therapist from the program, came to our house each week and worked on developing David's neck and core muscles. She explained that, until David developed those muscles, he would not be able to crawl, walk, or sit up.

One day, I was on the floor working with David when I noticed

Toby sitting on the perimeter of the rug. Maine coon cats are known to like being around people, but they aren't fond of curling up on people's laps and do not appreciate being held. Fascinated by the baby, Toby didn't move even a couple of inches away from David.

That day, I placed David on his stomach on top of an inflatable inclined pillow (a wedge) to get him to practice lifting his head up and turning it from side to side. Toby walked in front of David, brushing his tail against the baby's face. David lifted his head and turned it to track Toby.

I watched in amazement while Toby continued to walk back and forth. Each time, the baby lifted his head slightly and followed the cat with his eyes, tracking Toby for only a second or less. As the days and weeks passed, though, David was able to hold his head up longer and move it from side to side when Toby crossed in front of him.

Our next step in therapy was to get David to reach for objects. As he lay on his stomach wedge, Diane would set a toy in front of him within his reach. Then she would hold his hand and make him touch the toy, repeating these steps for both hands. She explained to me that as most children develop, they naturally sit up or reach for objects. However, children with Down's and other disabilities, which affect core muscles, tend not to have that natural instinct and must be taught in incremental steps.

During the following weeks, I worked with David to get him to reach for objects. Again, Toby walked in front and sat next to him, just out of his reach. Then one day while he sat next to David, I noticed Toby's tail flipping up and down. As David tracked the cat's tail, I helped him reach for it. Toby allowed David to grasp his tail. When David pulled on it slightly, he batted him with his paw but did not use his claws. Then he moved farther away but remained still within David's view.

As the days and weeks passed, Toby became accustomed to

David pulling his fur, ears, and tail. Never once did the cat scratch David or bite him. My only thought was, who could have known that Toby would play such a vital role in David's development? It was such a pleasant surprise and unexpected source of therapy.

Eight months passed, and we added cognitive and speech therapy to David's regimen. Toby remained by his side. It was at this time that my youngest daughter, Kathryn, began to have more frequent asthma attacks. We figured it was cold-induced asthma prompted by the changing season. When her asthma persisted, we finally had her tested for allergies.

Her blood work came back showing that Kathryn was severely allergic to cats and dogs. This broke our hearts. Toby was family. He had helped David so patiently and lovingly. We didn't know what to do.

In a few months, Kathryn had a severe asthma attack that necessitated partial bed rest for a week. I knew then that Toby would have to leave our home. I posted a notice on Facebook, saying that I was looking for a good home for him. I asked friends at the school where I teach if they knew of anyone who would love to adopt Toby. When all that failed, a friend told me to post a notice on Craigslist about Toby's need for adoption.

I didn't want to do it, but at this point I had run out of options. I knew I did not want to send loyal Toby to an animal shelter. I had to find a home for him; I could not keep my daughter's health in jeopardy. On Craigslist, I posted an ad detailing Toby's need for a new home, and immediately I got emails from people I did not know. They warned me to be careful about people who answered ads for small animals. Some unscrupulous people were looking for domestic cats to train dogs for dog fighting. They told me to beware of people who might want a cat for laboratory testing. That night, I cried myself to sleep and prayed for help in doing the right thing for Toby.

The next day, I got three emails from people who said they were interested in adopting Toby. One was a single male, and the second one was a man who claimed to be looking for a Maine coon for his wife as a gift. The warnings in the other emails immediately made me suspicious of the first two email responses, and I paid close attention to my intuition. The last email was from a lady who said that her sister had seen a Maine coon cat at a pet supply store near their home but could not afford the one hundred dollar adoption fee. Her sister had four children. Two of them had a blood disorder, and the sister's five-year-old son had autism.

I immediately sent a reply to the woman and gave her my personal email address and my cell phone number. Within minutes, my phone rang, and we talked for about ten minutes. The next day, the woman's sister called, and we talked for a long time, as if we had known each other forever.

On the Wednesday before Thanksgiving, the family who wanted to adopt Toby drove to my house and sat in my living room. My daughters helped me hold Toby, so the children in the family could pet him. They promised to give him the love and care he deserved.

With a heavy heart I placed Toby in the cat carrier and listened to him cry. It was one of the hardest things I'd ever had to do. Gently I took him to his new family's car. My daughters and I waved good-bye and watched Toby leave to begin his new life with another family that also had children with special needs.

After they drove away and we went inside the house, we broke down and cried uncontrollably. We each dealt with separation from Toby in our own way. Kathryn and my other daughter, Sarah, went to their respective rooms and cried themselves to sleep and would not eat all day. I cried and cradled David close to me, knowing that he was too young to understand how important Toby had been to his development.

Shortly after Toby left, I sent an email to the woman who had adopted Toby, asking how he had adjusted. She assured me that the children absolutely loved him, and that he was doing well in his new environment. Apparently, Toby was the topic of grateful discussion during Thanksgiving dinner. We all had something to be thankful for that day.

David will be two years old in April. Although he is still behind for his age cognitively and developmentally, he is progressing at his own pace. I marvel at how much he grows each week. I will always be grateful to Toby for giving David a reason to lift up his head and reach out to his unlikely source of therapy.

Meditation

Sometimes, someone bears watching because he or she is making you pay attention to what is important. Has observing an animal taught you anything?

The Turkey Who Helped
a Blind Teenager Find Her Song

Ellie Laks, SANTA CLARITA, CALIFORNIA

"Julia" was born to sing. She sang and twirled like a ballerina
from the time she could walk, even though she was blind from
birth. She had a joy about her that was refreshing and unusual. In
1994, when Julia was six years old, the big earthquake that shook
Los Angeles rocked her world. I guess being blind and helpless
traumatized her more than anyone could have imagined. Her parents and teachers tried for years to get her to speak, but she did not
say a word after the earthquake. Ever.

After the earthquake, Julia also had temper tantrums at home
and at school. She would scratch, bite, and kick anyone nearby. Julia
was an island, living in her own world, in her own mind. She was
usually parked in front of the television at home. At school she did
not have friends or interact with anyone other than her aide, who
would shadow her to make sure she caused no harm to anyone else.

When I first met Julia, she was seventeen years old and withdrawn. She sat with her eyes closed, rocking back and forth as if to
soothe herself. She seemed a little out of it, not present. She was tall
for her age and had pale blond hair. Her face was beautiful like an
angel's.

Julia came to The Gentle Barn with her special needs class. The
Gentle Barn is home to 130 animals recovering from abuse. We have
horses, cows, pigs, goats, sheep, llamas, turkeys, chickens, peacocks,
emus, dogs, cats, a donkey, and a parrot. Once the animals are

34

healed, they stay with us for the rest of their lives and help us heal at-risk inner-city kids, and kids with special needs, who come to the barn. Through interaction with the animals, the children learn kindness, compassion, and confidence.

On Julia's first visit to The Gentle Barn, kids were holding chickens and petting other animals. When I approached her with a red hen named Bonnie, the teachers yelled at me in front of Julia, telling me to stop. They explained that the hen would not be safe with the teenager, because Julia was prone to violence. Julia stayed completely withdrawn and showed no reaction to their warning. I looked over at her and noticed her sweet face. She did not seem like a threat to me, and I wanted to give her a chance. The teachers kept advising against it, but I insisted on taking the risk, and they relented.

Like the sun rising and illuminating the darkness, a smile spread across Julia's lonely, troubled face when I placed Bonnie in her arms. She stroked the chicken for hours, not wanting to put her down. She was gentle and kind the whole time. Julia treated the hen like a precious China doll.

The teachers were amazed at Julia's tenderness with the chicken that day, but they still thought I was crazy not to heed their warnings. They believed it was only a matter of time until the girl hurt one of our animals.

Julia started looking forward to coming to The Gentle Barn. Her counselors told me that the minute the teenager heard that she would be coming here, she would burst into a huge smile. I watched her through the windows of the bus as it arrived. She would be still and quiet, but when the bus doors opened and Julia heard the roosters crow, she would grin once again. She came two times a month with her class, and whenever she visited our place she was never violent or angry. Her teachers were amazed, because the girl's rages continued everywhere else. But after years of watching her out-of-control anger, they were seeing a different side of Julia, at peace with the animals, and they began to trust her. That is what The Gentle Barn is all about — giving second chances.

Julia loved all the animals at the barn, but I wanted to find one she could especially relate to, one who would encourage her to come out of her shell. I thought the ideal animal for her to work with would be our turkey Chloe. When I first had this idea, I did not know what a perfect match Chloe would be for a blind, angry girl who had lost her voice.

In 2004 we had rescued Chloe from a market where anyone can pick out which turkey they want. A person on the sales staff takes the turkey in the back and kills it, and the customer takes the bird home. We took Chloe home alive and unharmed to be our baby instead of someone's Thanksgiving dinner. Her toes and beak had been cut off with a hot blade, and she was filthy dirty.

After we cleaned her up, we discovered that Chloe was white as snow with deep, soulful black eyes. She had beautiful little pink bumps on her head and neck, which were meant to serve like jewelry and make her attractive to other turkeys. She came to The Gentle Barn an angry bird, and we thought she would hate people her whole life. To our surprise, after four weeks she would climb into our laps and fall asleep.

The rescued turkey became a hero and a role model of forgiveness for the foster kids and the ones on probation with whom we work. Many of them are inspired by Chloe's story because they too are working on forgiveness and trying to move on with their lives. The younger children, particularly those around eleven or twelve, always raise their hands and say that they understand how Chloe must have felt. They say they were hurt by a mother, father, or stepparent and are trying to forgive them. They want to be able to accept the love they are receiving now from counselors, foster parents, and other supportive people in their lives.

Chloe eventually became a regular part of the many fairs we attended. When the kids would arrive at our booth, she did her job, allowing them to pet and hold her. We always had a booth at a fair in Los Angeles called WorldFest, an annual vegan event featuring music, food, beauty products, and booths that encourage a vegan, cruelty-free lifestyle. The fair organizers invite us to help children make connections with animals they don't usually get to meet. One year, we decided to take Chloe with us. She sat quietly on the grass as we prepared our booth with tables and tents.

Our booth was about fifty feet from a stage being set up for performers. The group that eventually started playing music was a six-piece country-blues band. It was perfect for family fun. The stage was very large, and space in front of it had been reserved for people who wanted to dance. Behind the dance space were rows of chairs where an audience could sit and enjoy the music.

All of a sudden Chloe sprang to her feet and ran toward the stage as the musicians played. She stood directly in front of the band and began swaying back and forth to the music. I did not notice any reaction from the band, but the audience loved it. They smiled, pointed, laughed, and enjoyed dancing with our turkey.

By then, visitors were arriving at our booth, and Chloe was supposed to be on hand for the children, so I ushered the dancing turkey back to our area. But the minute I turned away, she ran back to her dance spot in front of the stage. This happened a couple more times, until I finally gave up. I sat and watched my turkey dance and sway with her eyes closed, almost in a trance. There were lots of people dancing around her, and she just joined in.

I was thinking, This is crazy. What is going on here? We have a job to do at our booth. Why won't she cooperate? It took me a while to realize what was really happening: in that moment, Chloe was getting the joy she needed. We stayed by the stage until lunch, when the band took a break. The minute the music stopped, Chloe opened her eyes, stopped dancing, and walked back to work at our booth.

After seeing that day how important music was to Chloe, we had a radio set up in the barn. From then on, wherever music played, Chloe danced, eyes half-closed, swaying to the rhythm. She loved all kinds of music and seemed to drift into a trance or meditate while listening. She could never get enough of it.

With their shared love of music and their past traumas, I realized, Chloe and Julia would be perfect for each other. The two had met before, because we introduce all our animals to the kids. But for the first time, I pulled Julia aside, on her own, to visit with Chloe one on one. I started by sitting with Julia while holding the bird on my lap. I told Julia that Chloe loved music, so it was important that we sing to her. I sang softly while Julia petted her.

Ellie's Chloe with Ellie's daughter, Cheyanne

Julia loved Chloe, as she did all the animals. Right away, she began petting her. I showed how to scratch Chloe under her wings and on her chest, which were her favorite places. At Julia's gentle touch, the turkey threw her head back and bit the air with her beak. This let us know that Julia had hit the right spot; it's much like the way a dog kicks his hind leg in reaction to a well-placed tummy scratch. I sang the Joe Cocker song "You Are So Beautiful" while Julia listened and petted Chloe.

From then on, every time Julia came to the barn, we repeated this process: I sang to Chloe while Julia petted her. Then it happened. One day, Julia began to hum along to the music. At first, she only hummed under her breath, almost inaudibly. But this child, who had lived blind and voiceless, was now making sounds.

Wow, I thought, Julia has been hiding from the world and herself all these years, and at last she is coming out to hum for a turkey. When Julia first came to The Gentle Barn, she was still traumatized from her experience with the earthquake. Her silence caused most of the people in her life to believe that she could not function normally. Because of her rages, they thought she wasn't capable of controlling her emotions. The teachers treated her like she was crazy and unpredictable. But I treated her like she was smart and let her know that I believed she wouldn't harm the animals. As a result, she let Chloe and me see that she was intelligent, brave, and beautiful.

It had taken only one person and one turkey to reveal Julia's true self. I felt honored to be with her for this breakthrough. Her face softened as Chloe sat on her lap, accepting the love within Julia's humming and giving it back.

After that day when Julia found her song, and during the next two years until she graduated from our program, Julia continued to heal. She became a different child, unlike the silent, sad, closed off, shut down, angry teen who had first entered our doors. Long gone were the days when her teachers warned me that Julia would be a danger to our animals if I let her handle them. Our staff trusted Julia to always be gentle.

She said hello to us when she arrived and good-bye upon leaving. She hugged us and the cows and insisted on being first to lead the horses around the property, and then did so with confidence and pride. Smiles of achievement lit up her face. Her teachers told us that the farm was the only place Julia had never had a tantrum.

Julia left us with a permanent smile on her face. By the time she graduated from high school, she was fully vocal like anyone else. With help from The Gentle Barn, both Julia and Chloe found their songs.

Meditation

Who are the dancing turkeys calling forth your songs? When will you be ready to let go of fear and sing them?

Justice for Children with Golden Caitee

Carolyn C. Corbett, WESTMINSTER, COLORADO

In 1998, I was thinking about what I still wanted to accomplish in my life. Since I love police work and dogs, I aspired to become a K9 officer. As I began to get experience going on ride-alongs with police officers that year, I took great pride in being involved in bringing criminals to justice and helping to meet the needs of my community. Volunteering as a victim advocate at Westminster Police Department (WPD) in Jefferson and Adams counties in Colorado was a natural fit. By the fall of that year, I completed the Victim Advocate Academy and began an incredible journey on which I did crisis intervention for children who must go through the difficult and confusing court process.

On Tuesday morning, April 20, 1999, I was at the WPD checking out my equipment bag for an evening shift when an emergency request for help came through. The Jefferson Sheriff's Department had sent out a call for crisis-response assistance from the WPD SWAT Team, asking for extra patrol officers and victim advocates. That's how I became one of the first responders to the tragedy at Columbine High School.

I had never seen so much chaos and trauma. I hope and pray there will never be anything that horrific ever again. During the hours I spent working in the aftermath of the Columbine shootings, I got the idea of having a trained therapy dog at my side to assist in crisis intervention. As a survivor of domestic violence myself, I knew firsthand that the power of canine companionship can save a person's life. Many times, my dog was my only source of unconditional love and support. I deeply understood the intricate personalities of both victims and dogs and how positively and effectively canines can help victims during and after traumatic events. In the years since Columbine, I've wondered what might have happened had a therapy dog been with me to ease the impact on the teenagers and adults who had to cope with the most shocking high school violence in our country's history.

In spring 2001, a seven-week-old golden retriever puppy came into my life, and I named her Caitlyn; her call name became Caitee. She was the pick of the litter — intelligent, precocious, inquisitive, and feisty. She was so rambunctious and energetic that, during the first ten days after her arrival, I was not sure I could keep her. The problem turned out to be me. I was making the mistake of separating Caitlyn and our older golden retriever, Chelsea. Once I let Chelsea teach Caitlyn the hierarchy in our family, everything was fine with our new puppy.

Shortly after bringing Caitlyn home, I enrolled her in obedience training. Somehow she knew which day of the week we went to class. On training days Caitee would go to the door leading to the garage, where her leashes hung, and would flip them with her nose. Then she would try to get my attention by running back and forth between the door and me. Because of her passion to learn and perform, we never stopped attending classes. Caitee started winning ribbons, medallions, and American Kennel Club titles for her accomplishments in AKC performance sports that required obedience and agility. Also, Caitee was compassionate and people oriented. She would seek people out to say hello.

When she was four and a half years old, an injury to Caitee's left shoulder, sustained while competing in agility trials, changed the course of our life's journey together. After Caitee's injury, I took an inventory of my life and asked myself, "What am I waiting for?" I realized I could combine my experience as a victim advocate with this special angel who could become a great therapy dog.

Within several months, I completed the workshop for therapy dog handlers, as required of those who want to become part of a registered therapy-dog team. The second requirement was that Caitee and I had to pass a rigorous aptitude and skills evaluation, which she and I did together. Then, so that the WPD would come to appreciate the merit of my idea to pair Caitee and me as victim advocates, my dog and I began volunteering at the University of Colorado Hospital's Inpatient Rehabilitation Unit, where we gained experience in animal-assisted therapy.

Having earned registration of our therapy dog team and gained several months of valuable experience, I decided it was time to present my ideas to the command staff at the WPD. Initially they were reserved, because there were no precedents in the state of Colorado upon which to base their decision. They were interested, but had lots of questions about how the program I was proposing would work. They were concerned about letting a dog run around the department, and they wanted to be sure they incurred no unexpected expenses. Police dogs were not allowed in the building, yet the WPD command staff approved a new policy that allowed therapy dogs to enter. I worked through their questions and concerns by developing a protocol and policies. It was my opportunity to educate the command staff about the benefits that would result from having a therapy dog as part of their team.

By the end of 2007, the WPD approved my proposed program to include a therapy-dog team in the WPD Victim Services Unit. Within a year, K9 c.a.r.e.s. (Canine Assisted Reduction of Eventful Stress) Victim Support became an integrated part of the WPD

Victim Services Unit as the first K9 support team for law enforcement in Colorado. The command staff of WPD and the Victim
Services Unit were about to discover that the most effective way
to lessen the impact of violence on children who were victims of
or witnesses to crimes would be to make use of low-tech, healing
puppy love.

Caitee's Special Mission

After we received the go-ahead, Caitee and I were on call 24-7 for
WPD emergencies. As the first K9 c.a.r.e.s. Victim Support team,
we began supporting victims and witnesses of many types of trag-
edies, including domestic violence, sexual assault, and murder. But
perhaps Caitee's greatest contribution has been the help she gives
children at our local child advocacy center after forensic interviews.
Detectives conduct forensic interviews to collect facts about crimes,
and it can be emotionally stressful for victims or witnesses to retell
their stories. Caitee waits for these children to exit the interviews
and greets them with a wagging tail. I engage the children in activities such as brushing Caitee, reading books to her, or playing games
with her. The children leave after having had fun with Caitee, who
takes their minds off the difficult events.

We also regularly visit a local shelter for women and children
who have been victims of domestic violence, where Caitee brings
comfort to the youngest casualties of shattered homes. Family Tree's
Women In Crisis Shelter was a refuge for "Rose," a very special little
five-year-old girl, and her mother. Because of the traumatic events
that they had survived, Rose remained locked in a dark and painful silence. When the mother and daughter walked into the room,
Rose, barely holding her head up, looked only at the floor.

Caitee relaxed her body but did not move a muscle. Slowly I

extended my hand in which I held a soft brush that had a red heart in the center of the bristles. I asked Rose if she would like to brush Caitee. She reached out and took the brush from me without making eye contact. I demonstrated how to brush Caitee's back. My gentle dog stayed still, letting Rose carefully approach her.

Rose brushed Caitee for over thirty minutes while I talked to her as if she were carrying on a conversation with me. The traumatized, fearful little girl remained completely silent. She had not spoken in days. Caitee's eyes lit up, the corners of her mouth pulled back into a smile, and it was as if she were looking into Rose's soul.

Caitee and her friend Gracie

Caitee continued to smile and even gently kissed Rose's hand. Rose began to sense that she was safe with Caitee. At first, I caught only a glimpse of a smile that indicated the child was feeling less tense. Then she laughed. Within the next few moments, Rose started talking excitedly about Caitee. Her protective silence had melted in the caring and warmth of a sensitive golden retriever's love.

Caitee's Days in Court

Caitee and I frequently provide services for the Seventeenth Judicial District's Fast Track Prosecution Program, which is used when a person is arrested and charged with domestic violence. The Fast Track program was established to protect families and quickly get them help. A private waiting room for victims and witnesses is housed in the district attorney's offices at the courthouse. It is usually filled with victims, witnesses, and their families waiting to talk about their cases and for their hearings to begin. Effortlessly, Caitee provides comfort and helps to ease the stress that accompanies difficult court days. Often, we are assigned to support the children, teens, or adults involved in a specific case. Caitee supports the victims and their families at various points in the criminal justice process by turning exhausting tasks into more positive (pawsitive) experiences.

When Caitee arrives at her destination, she dons her vest, which bears an official photo ID badge. I can tell that the vest is her signal that it is time for her to go to work, because Caitee's demeanor switches to professional mode. She takes great pride in helping others as she sits up straight with her head held high and chest pushed out. She focuses intensely on everything happening in the room. Her intelligence, calm demeanor, loving nature, and innate ability to sense emotion have an instant effect on victims. She helps the walls of the police department or the courthouse melt away for them.

Caitee studies human behavior by waiting, watching, and matching her manner to what she senses children need at the moment. This amazing orchestration allows her to determine what approach to take to heal someone. I trust her instincts implicitly. She goes to a person and leans her head gently against the side of his or her knee to assess something. I don't know what she senses, but intuitively she knows who needs her most. She continues to work the room, returning to folks who are still emotional, until everyone's spirits have improved. She is not happy until they all feel better.

In December 2008 the Denver district attorney's office suggested to an attorney that he request Caitee's assistance with a difficult case. "Johnnie," a five-year-old boy, was having a hard time talking about the horrifying abuse he had suffered at the hands of his father. As soon as Caitee met the child, the two of them became good buddies, smiling back and forth at each other as if in a smiling contest.

Before the father's court date, the attorney filed a motion with the Denver juvenile court to permit my K9 c.a.r.e.s. Victim Support team to accompany Johnnie into the judge's chambers and stay with the child during the little boy's testimony. On December 17, 2008, at the last minute, the judge approved the motion.

When Johnnie arrived in the judge's waiting room at the Denver County Court, the boy lit up at the sight of a wonderful doggy welcoming committee. Johnnie played with his furry friend while waiting for the proceedings to begin. This helped keep him relaxed and distracted him from his anxiety over having to testify against his father.

Caitee and her friend Joshua

I gave Johnnie a small, colorful leash for Caitee. When the time came for testimony to begin, Johnnie, with the leash in his hand, walked proudly next to Caitee into the chambers. She obeyed his commands to sit, stop, come, stay, and jump up. The young victim took his place at the judge's conference table, while Caitee sat in a chair next to him. The staff placed a bowl of water on the table at Caitee's place.

Throughout his testimony, Johnnie held tightly to Caitee's leash. Her presence gave him the confidence to talk to the court officials. Having Caitee by his side empowered this child victim during a frightening proceeding that required him to answer uncomfortable questions. During the hearing, the one thing Johnnie had control of was Caitee. Her calming companionship had the extra benefit of comforting Johnnie's distressed foster mother. Without Caitee, Johnnie could have been as anxious and nervous as his foster mother was when she had first arrived.

When it was time to leave, Johnnie thanked both of us and gave Caitee a big neck hug and several kisses on her forehead. It was an image I will always remember. On that cold December morning, Caitee had done more than warm people's hearts. She had made Colorado court history by being the first therapy dog to accompany a child into a judge's chambers while the child gave testimony.

Caitee, the Healer

In February 2010, on sentencing day in court, a mother faced her husband, who, as a stepfather, had sexually abused her teenage daughter, "Abby." The victimization had gone on for many years before Abby's mother discovered the truth. Now Abby and her mother sat close together outside the courtroom, anxiously awaiting the conclusion of a very long, difficult court process.

The court's victim advocate and translator (the mother spoke predominately Spanish, while Abby spoke both English and Spanish) had asked if Caitee and I could be present on the sentencing date. Abby's mother, who had been attacked by a dog as a child and was still afraid of dogs, reluctantly agreed. Despite her own fears, the mother was positive that Caitee could help her daughter because the girl loved dogs. The mother wanted to speak to the judge at sentencing about what her now ex-husband had put her family through, even though she was terrified of being in the same room with the man.

After we introduced ourselves, Abby immediately became friends with Caitee. I could see the teenager become calm as she petted Caitee. The stress that had shown on her face turned into a smile. When the moment arrived for the court proceedings to begin, mother and daughter visibly trembled. The teenage victim did not want to go into the courtroom and face the convicted perpetrator; so she chose to wait outside the door and sit on a bench with Caitee and me.

Courageously, Abby's mother went into the courtroom and addressed the judge for about fifteen minutes. The court advocate explained to me that the mother boldly told the judge that her daughter's life had forever changed. Outside the courtroom door, Caitee helped to distract Abby from the proceedings. The judge's decision came swiftly. He sentenced the defendant to two consecutive life terms. Justice had been served, and the family's ordeal was over.

To my surprise, when the mother came out of the courtroom she ran straight over to Caitee and hugged her tightly. She and Abby cried into Caitee's fur for a long time. (Good thing Caitee is waterproof.) I placed a box of tissues in front of Caitee, and she gently pulled out a tissue and offered it to her tearful friend. Caitee did not judge, pull away, or ask questions, which is exactly what Abby and her mother needed. It was an honestly inspiring experience to watch my K9 friend empower this devastated family.

Caitee Continues Her Good Work with Children

At the end of the workday, Caitee is a very tired pup because she puts her whole heart into every visit. She gives so much to others that it is a pleasure when I have the opportunity to pamper her by playing ball with her, letting her get up on our couch, giving her a tummy rub, or letting her lick my oatmeal bowl. I make training fun, and as a result she knows more than one hundred verbal commands and hand signals. I incorporate her many commands into everyday life; they are practical and can be entertaining to others.

We also work with a children's literacy program, the Reading Education Assistance Dogs (R.E.A.D.) program at the College Hill Library, one of Westminster's public libraries. Caitee is a registered R.E.A.D. dog. She helped develop a children's literacy program named K9 c.a.r.e.s. about READ'ing at College Hill Library in Westminster. Reading to Caitee helps children focus on their reading and improves their self-confidence because she does not criticize or make corrections. Caitee creates a safe environment for children to practice their skills. Her gentle attention and wagging tail encourage them to discover the true joy of reading.

Our dedicated ambitions have come to fruition as the community embraces our amazing work. My nonprofit organization, K9 c.a.r.e.s. Victim Support, is now developing affiliated programs in other agencies across Colorado. Caitee and I have been training twelve more therapy dog teams so they can be certified to do the same sort of work we do. We pioneered a new field for animal-assisted therapy service and remain engaged in our groundbreaking work in law enforcement and the criminal justice system. I know one district judge at the Adams County court who frequently says, "Victim advocates do the work of angels." I believe the truly angelic work is done by an angel disguised as a golden retriever named Caitee.

In April 2010, Caitee and I were honored as the recipients of the esteemed Thomas E. Green Award for outstanding service to victims in Colorado's Seventeenth Judicial District. That same year, the American Kennel Club also selected Caitee for honorable mention in the therapy dog category of its Awards for Canine

Excellence. Caitee brings healing to many as she helps child victims get through some of the most difficult moments of their lives.

Meditation

Children who are frightened need advocates. How could you help others know that justice is served better with the help of a caring canine?

Peter Pan's Nana Became My Daughters' Playmate

Linda Freedman, CHESHIRE, CONNECTICUT

We had always been a two-dog family, and all of our dogs were rescues. To see two rescued dogs romping together in the yard warms my heart, and I know that we have made a difference in the dogs' lives, too. Some came to us from shelters; some came after we contacted people who had been featured in stories in our local newspaper describing a need for new homes for their dogs.

One day, shortly after we lost our border collie mix, Chelsea, to cancer, someone we knew, who was also a friend of a woman who had rescued a puppy, called and asked if we could foster the now five-year-old dog. Jessica, the dog, was a medium-sized black Labrador-terrier cross. The woman's health was deteriorating, and she had prayed that Jessica would find a new home before she passed on.

My husband, Bob, and I had been thinking of adopting another rescued dog. There was a definite hole in the fabric of our lives without Chelsea. I discussed Jessica's situation with Bob and our four-year-old daughter, Erica. Even at her tender age, Erica felt that our other dog, Felicity, a white shepherd mix, missed Chelsea. Just as people have best friends, dogs do too, I think, and Felicity and Chelsea had been great buddies. Erica said, "Mommy, Tee Tee is sad." From the look on Erica's face, I knew that Tee Tee (Felicity) wasn't the only sad one.

Erica loved to stand in the yard, wave her arms, and yell, "Run!"

At this command, both Felicity and Chelsea would look at each other and take off in a race, nipping playfully at one another. This would send Erica into fits of giggles. Now that Chelsea was gone, Erica could no longer enjoy their dog races.

My biggest reservation about taking in Jessica was that, although I had experience with fostering cats and kittens, I had not fostered a dog. With the understanding that fostering her would be temporary, and since we had room for one more dog, we agreed to accept responsibility for Jessica. We would adopt another dog later, after she was settled into a new home with a loving family.

Jessica's New Home

The woman who had found the puppy Jessica near a Dumpster, searching for food, was extremely allergic to dogs. She gave Jessica everything a dog could ask for except the comfort of living inside a home. Jessica came indoors for daily visits with the woman for short periods of time, but then returned to her well-insulated doghouse in the yard.

After Jessica arrived at our home, she had to cope all at once with a whole new set of circumstances that were vastly different from those of her life up to that point. She had lived quietly with one person, no children, and no other animals. We, on the other hand, were two adults, a young child, a dog, and two cats — Schwartz, a large black-and-white tuxedo cat, and Snowy, a white cat with bright blue eyes.

Erica had learned how to welcome new animals into our house from participating in my work with fostering cats and kittens. She was careful to let our new arrivals adjust and not try to touch them until they were ready. Felicity and Chelsea had been part of our family before Erica was born, and I think she felt they were more ours than hers. Upon the new foster dog's arrival, Erica told me with smiling eyes, "Jessica will be *my* dog."

There is only so much restraint a young child can muster when welcoming a new dog she hopes will be her special friend, so Erica was especially eager to be Jessica's welcoming committee. The dog remained unperturbed by Erica's enthusiastic greeting. Erica asked me to take her shopping, and she chose a new brush and bowl for the dog. That first night, she donated one of her baby blankets for Jessica to sleep on and arranged it carefully on the floor next to her bed.

Upon her arrival Jessica and Felicity sniffed each other with their tails wagging. Felicity seemed genuinely pleased to have another dog in the house again. Jessica's first reaction to the cats, though, was to chase them. I gave her a stern "No!" She seemed to understand right away that the cats were off-limits.

Erica and Jessica

During her first day with us, Jessica urinated on the living room rug a couple of times. I brought her to our veterinarian the next day for a checkup, and he assured me that she was a healthy dog. He advised that her accidents were probably due to the stress of the move.

I decided to give Jessica extra attention and quiet time with me. Erica was in morning nursery school three days a week, which gave Jessica and me time to spend alone together. I would sit on the floor and call her to me. She would trot over with her tail in constant motion, flop down, and place her head on my lap. I would speak softly to her while stroking her side and gently scratching behind her ears. Eventually, the tail would stop wagging and she'd fall asleep. Her soiling accidents soon stopped.

Jessica and Felicity never had a harsh moment with each·other. Maybe one rescued dog instinctively senses another. The two dogs played well together. Jessica's gift to Erica was the trait of her breed — she loved to retrieve. Whenever Felicity fetched a ball, she would drop it where she stood. We'd tried to teach her to bring the ball back to us, but she had never caught on. To a four-year-old who throws wild pitches, it was a blessing to have a dog who never tired of chasing balls all over the yard. Sometimes, much to Erica's delight, Jessica would dash into the garden and bring back a tomato instead of a ball.

The two dogs made up a new game. They entertained Erica with a stick tug-of-war. Erica would choose a sturdy stick and toss it. Both dogs would grab on to an end of the stick and run around the yard, each one trying to end up in possession of the treasure. They added some play growling for realism, which made Erica laugh out loud. She was delighted that we were a two-dog family again.

Our days with Jessica turned into weeks, and it became clear that she was a perfect fit for our family. One day as I watched Erica and the dogs in the yard, I realized we had found our second dog. I asked Bob if he agreed, and he did. Jessica and the cats were getting along fine; after that one earlier reprimand, she had understood not to chase them. They, too, seemed to realize that she was part of the family.

I really didn't think I had to ask Erica if Jessica should stay, because it was clear how happy the new dog had made her. But I did ask, so I could have the pleasure of hearing her reaction.

I called Erica to our back door, and as usual Jessica came too and stood only a step behind her. "Would you like Jessica to be our dog?" I asked. Erica jumped up and down, shouting, "Yes! Yes!" Jessica sensed the joy in the little girl and began to do a doggy happy dance behind her. Erica turned, knelt in front of Jessica, and gave her a tight squeeze around the neck. "You're going to live here!" Jessica was home to stay.

Jessica's Many Roles

Jessica quickly found her calling, one of her many roles — a position that Felicity had not filled for our daughter. For Erica, an only child, Jessica became a surrogate sister. One of her assignments was to be a regular guest at Erica's tea parties, where she happily slurped water out of child-sized cups and nibbled bits of cookies from tiny plastic plates.

Jessica, the only guest, happily anticipated the ritual of Erica's tea. She sat patiently on the floor on her special tea party mat with her tail wagging. She never took anything before Erica offered it, showing manners that would impress Emily Post. Tea parties require the proper attire, and Erica was ready to supply it. She treasured a box of her grandmother's costume jewelry, with its long strands of beads. Jessica was such a good sport that she even allowed Erica to clip earrings to her ears.

I also saw another role that Jessica played for my daughter: that of Nana, the dog in the Peter Pan story who was always vigilant and ever loving. Jessica spent hours with Erica sitting on blankets in large cardboard boxes in the backyard. While some dogs might be intimidated by a big cardboard box, Jessica was happy to lie in one all afternoon. The large boxes created many scenes in my child's imagination. Erica always kept a bowl of kibble nearby to serve as pretend survival food whenever the box served as their fort. When it was a box library, she would bring books in and read to

Jessica. Sometimes a box served as their house or their hideout. Or it became a simple shelter to shade them from the sun on a summer day.

Jessica was patient when Erica brushed her fur in the wrong direction or adorned the dog with multiple necklaces. Erica discovered that, with a bit of stretching, she could get a T-shirt on the dog. Although Jessica didn't seem to mind, as evidenced by her nonstop tail wagging, I never let this dog dressing and accessorizing go on for too long. Truly, though, Jessica was willing to do anything to please Erica.

One afternoon, I was out in the garden and left Jessica and Erica playing together briefly while I went back in the house to watch television. Erica didn't want to risk Jessica getting sunburned. Since I made Erica wear sunscreen, she thought Jessica needed it, too. I returned to the garden to find this sweet dog sitting perfectly still while my daughter slathered her with sunscreen.

Jessica Plus Two

The year after we adopted Jessica, our daughter Emily was born. Jessica now divided her time between the two children. For five hours a day, she watched over the baby while Erica was in school. Wherever I was in the house, Jessica slept by my feet but stayed alert for Emily's cry. She always made it up the stairs before I did and sat looking into the crib, her tail wagging in anticipation of my lifting Emily out of it.

After I gave Jessica a chance to check Emily with a concerned sniff, we would go downstairs. I'd place Emily on a blanket on the floor. Jessica knew, without my instruction, not to lie on the blanket. Instead, she got as close as possible, with her nose merely touching the blanket, and tried to will the baby over to the edge.

This ploy often worked. After Erica came home each day, Jessica returned to being a willing participant in her games.

Emily learned to walk when she was fourteen months old. The toddler sometimes stepped on Jessica's toes or grabbed handfuls of fur around her neck to hoist herself up so she could stand. Jessica never showed annoyance but always stayed patient and helpful.

Once Emily was mobile, she kept Jessica busy. Jessica followed Emily through the house. Each time Emily stumbled and sat on the floor, Jessica encouraged the baby with a lick on the face. She was never startled by the screechy outbursts that toddlers emit. Although I tried to intervene in every instance, Emily would at times joyously bop Jessica on the head with a toy. Jessica would continue to wag her tail and respond with love. I was amazed. For a dog who had not interacted with small, unpredictable beings before coming into our home, she did remarkably well with the movements of an erratic toddler.

Jessica recognized the sound of the school bus and waited by the door at exactly the right time. She would do her little happy dance, tapping her feet as she watched Erica step off the bus. When Erica saw Jessica, her face brightened, and all the little troubles of the school day vanished. Jessica seemed relieved each day when her child returned from wherever she had gone. Erica's safe arrival meant that Jessica could settle down for a nap.

Erica and Emily shared a bedroom, and Jessica slept on her own dog bed between their beds. After the girls were in their pajamas, but before they went to sleep at night, they would each read a story to her. She never tired of their endless readings of Dr. Seuss books. Sometimes the girls would tiptoe out of their bedroom and report to us, giggling, that Jessica had fallen asleep while listening to their bedtime stories.

Jessica was a happy camper during summer afternoons spent in tents that Erica and Emily made from sheets fastened to the top of the swing set. All the children who came to visit us loved Jessica. She befriended them by sitting quietly so they could pet her for hours while she looked up at them with her deep, soulful eyes.

She was the guest of honor at the girls' sleepover parties. Many children didn't have a dog at home. Jessica's willingness to give 100 percent of her love immediately made each of the girls beg the dog to come to her next. From our bedroom, I could hear the girls downstairs pleading with her to sleep by them. Jessica gladly spent the night moving from one sleeping bag to the next.

Jessica and I shared some wonderful times together, too. We spent lovely afternoons walking in the woods around our house. Although she was not formally trained to walk off-leash, she always stayed close to me. If I sat, she sat. If I walked, she walked. Jessica was the calm spot in the happy chaos of my family life. I would point out a bird in a tree or a plant that looked interesting, knowing that she really didn't understand me. But she looked up, the ever-wagging tail telling me that she was happy to listen for as long as I wanted to talk to her.

Returning the Love

One winter afternoon, I heard Jessica whimpering in the kitchen. I raced to her side, worried that I would find her injured or sick. She was looking into the backyard with her nose pressed against the glass of the storm door, her front feet anxiously stomping up and down. She had smudged the glass as she tried to force the door open.

With her, I watched the playful scene of Erica and Emily sliding down the little snow-covered hill in our yard, squealing in mock terror. Clearly, Jessica was upset by what she witnessed through the glass. I opened the door, and she bolted out to rescue the children. Tenderly she licked their faces to comfort them. Having grown so attached to the children, she must have considered them to be hers to help raise and protect. I wondered if she feared losing them as she had lost the woman who had rescued her.

By the time Jessica was twelve years old and had shared our lives for nearly seven years, her hips became too painful for her to walk. Up until then, she had been having more good days than bad, but now the bad were coming more often. The sparkle in her eyes had been replaced by a pleading look. I knew she was letting us know it was time. Bob knew it, too. The girls, eleven and five by then, also saw the pain in their faithful friend and protector.

Tearfully, we were all in agreement that we could not let such a wonderful friend suffer after all the unconditional love she had given us. Just as she had put us first for so long, we had to put her needs before our own. We decided that I would be the one to stay with Jessica as she passed. The girls went to school as usual but with their hearts heavy, knowing that their dear friend would not be there to greet them when they arrived home.

On the last day we would have with our children's precious companion, I carried Jessica to the car and placed her on her favorite blanket for the ride to the vet. My last loving act would be to free her from pain. I thanked her for taking care of us, as I stroked her soft fur for the last time.

Later that day, Jessica gently slipped away. Knowing that she had spent her last years living a life she loved eased my pain at her passing.

I feel that she rescued us as much as we rescued her. We had opened up our hearts and home to a dog in need, thinking that we were doing something wonderful for her. She became so much more than just a second dog in our home. She taught us about patience, kindness, and facing life with pure joy. She taught us to wake up and expect another day of fun. We watched her silliness, and we felt silly. She was our Nana, the loyal, protective, and above all, loving playmate and caretaker of all our childhood dreams.

Meditation

Who were your childhood pet playmates? Did they inspire you to love unconditionally and give without expecting a return?

My Child with Autism and the Dog Who Adores Her

Pam Thorsen, HASTINGS, MINNESOTA

She came on a cold, blustery winter night from the sickbed of her human companion, Dan. My husband and I wanted to be her forever family, but her nervousness led us to believe her heart remained with her best friend. She could no longer stay by Dan's side. He was moving into a hospice where he could not take her. We were most impressed with her loving attention to him. There obviously had been a special bond between them, and we knew how sad they would be without each other.

She shivered and looked worried. Even though she was only four years old, her little brow creased with what seemed like a permanent wrinkle. She was a German wire-haired pointer, black except for the perfect gray markings of her breed: gray beard, whiskers, and eyebrows, and gray feathered fur from her knees to her feet. Her name was Maya. We lengthened it to Maya Angel Ah, a playful variation on the name of our family's favorite author and poet, Maya Angelou.

It was weeks before Maya adjusted to our home. At first, she paced a lot and followed me everywhere, seldom relaxing. We soon learned that one of her fears was that she would be left outside. After Dan became terribly ill, he would let her outdoors and then would be unable to get back up to bring her inside. Minnesota winters can be very hard on a shorthaired dog. So although she was perfectly housetrained, when she asked to go out she raced back indoors after doing her business, fearing that she might be forgotten. Her terror was so great that, at first, when she left through the door, she walked backward into the yard, watching to be sure someone would be waiting for her. Light on her feet, Maya dashed in and out so fast that her feet hardly seemed to touch the ground.

When our daughter, Britty, was eighteen, Maya started following her around the house. Britty has autism and Down syndrome, is cognitively age six or seven, and does not have the use of language. Maya and Britty frequently stared into each other's eyes, and we imagined they were communicating. Their long gazes were a little unusual, because one of the traits of autism is the avoidance of eye contact. But at their first meeting Maya and Britty both did double takes, as if to say, "Hey, I know you."

Britty's habit of twirling ribbons and spinning things, another trait of autism, mesmerized Maya, who seemed almost catlike in her fascination with the movement. She often positioned her head beneath whatever Britty twirled and placed her nose on my daughter's lap. Now that Maya's wrinkled brow was smoother and she felt more secure, she occasionally swished her tail so that it touched Britty, much to Britty's delight. Perhaps the dog was reciprocating because of the special connection between them.

An interesting new aspect of Britty's focused twirling was that it became more purposeful and connected, which is unusual for a child with autism. In the past Britty had twirled objects in order to tune out the world. Now, she started making the twirling into a game to get Maya's attention. We saw marked improvement in our daughter's attentiveness to the world around her after she began to interact with Maya.

As Maya grew to love and trust her new family, she adjusted to being in the yard by herself. Tasks in Maya's day included the daily ritual of seeing that Britty got on the school bus. This dog is not a barker. So, from the middle of the fenced backyard on our corner lot facing the street, as the bus rounded the corner near our house and pulled into the driveway, she would do a perfect hunting point pose by straightening her feathered tail behind her, lifting one back leg off the ground, lengthening her neck, and pointing her nose at the bus. The kids on the bus and the driver loved it. After Britty got on the bus and it drove away, Maya would circle the yard, run into the house at lightning speed, drink thirstily, and fall to the floor, exhausted.

Maya and Britty

Just before 2:30 in the afternoon, Maya would pop up from one of her dog beds or the couch and run to the door, knowing full well that her sister was due to come home. She would race around the yard when the bus came, then switch from high gear to low, matching Britty's slow pace as she walked from the bus to the backyard gate, which opened automatically to let them in our yard.

Maya never left Britty's side when the two of them were outdoors. If Britty was on the swing, Maya lay beneath it. We found it amazing that the dog never got bumped or hit by the swing. If Britty played on the patio, Maya stretched out in the sun beside her. If Britty moved to the middle of the yard or onto the porch, Maya traveled by her side.

Inside, when Britty watched television shows or DVDs, Maya offered her companionship. Even though there was barely enough room for one of them in the window seat of Britty's room, Maya snuggled next to our daughter while she listened to music. We gave up trying to get Britty to stop giving scraps from the table at dinnertime to Maya, who fit perfectly under my daughter's chair, where she waited for the treats. Britty gave food to Maya with one hand while watching us peripherally. And of course, Maya always slept in bed with Britty.

The most comforting symbol of their connection and Maya's sensitive nature appeared when Britty would occasionally fall ill or otherwise not feel well. We knew right away if Britty was sick, because Maya stayed on the floor next to her bed and not *in* the bed. With her kind and gentle spirit, she seemed to know to let Britty have the bed to herself. But her furry, wrinkled brow remained exactly an arm's length away from Britty's tiny hand.

We are grateful for the nurturing love Maya Angel Ah gives Britty. We thought we were doing the rescuing when Dan could no longer keep her. But she has added an amazing dimension to our family as our daughter's constant companion. The changes we have noticed since Maya became part of our family include Britty's better eye contact and more focused attention, as well as the conversations we now have with our daughter. Britty even has a certain new skip to her step that we attribute to Maya's devotion. In fact, we are all skipping since Maya Angel Ah came into our lives.

Meditation

When a family needs canine intervention, how can a dog contribute to their hopefulness? Has a pet's devotion made a difference in your life?

PART TWO

....

Healing

Thuson of Hermione, a blind boy,
had his eyes licked in the daytime
by one of the dogs about the temple,
and departed cured.

— Inscription on a tablet at Epidaurus, a city in ancient Greece

The Kindness of Horses, Llamas, and Chickens

Tanya Welsch, SAINT PAUL, MINNESOTA

My love of nature nurtured me in ways I did not fully appreciate until I began my professional career, over twenty years ago, in the children's mental health field. I discovered that hospitalized youth had an easier time talking about their feelings if we went for a walk on the hospital grounds. And some of my clients would become different people altogether if I brought my dog to work. When I learned about a modality called animal-assisted interactions (AAI), I realized it would be a perfect fit for me.

I was pleasantly surprised to find that most of my clients had a current or past positive connection to a pet or other animal, which enabled the children and me to develop unique relationships. For example, when I visited the home of one family for the first time, one of the children was anxious to show me his pet. Of course, I was equally eager to see the animal. The child said his pet was named Fluffy, and I thought there could be no harm in meeting an animal with such a sweet name.

Before I knew what was happening, the child had placed on my shoulder a large white rat who proceeded to leave a few stinky presents there. The entire family waited for my response, likely thinking I would scream and run out of the house. When I picked up Fluffy, stroked him on his back, and remarked about what a fine-looking rat he was, I passed this family's test. Our therapy together could begin.

Laura Rides on Ellie's Wings

"Laura" and I started working together because she didn't fit in at school and had a hard time focusing in class. She was often bullied, had few friends, and believed that even the teachers didn't like her. Her mother noticed Laura slowly sinking into depression and making little effort to have a social life. The family's dog was Laura's only friend.

Laura resisted the idea of counseling until I explained that my nonprofit organization, Natural Connections Learning Center, would offer her AAI. Since I am a licensed, credentialed mental health practitioner, I can use AAI as a form of therapy for my clients. I prefer it because it acts as a gentle catalyst, helping a child to focus on learning and developing social and emotional skills. I work with various animal species in AAI. Ideally, as has happened in my case, both the human and the animal team members receive specialized training together and pass a nationally recognized evaluation of their competency and their suitability to provide AAI.

During Laura's initial meeting with me at the Natural Connections Learning Center, she expressed her lifelong goal to learn to ride horses. Laura's was not the wish of a young girl with fantasies of her hair streaming in the wind as she rides atop a mighty steed. Instead, she expressed a desire for horses to relieve her of sadness and pain. "I wish I was a horse so I could ride away from my life," she said.

We started with the basics of learning about and caring for horses, in particular for Ellie, the paint horse Laura would be working with. Ellie was coal black except for her four white socks, a large white blaze, and a small bit of white in her tail. Each week, Laura and I walked out to the pasture to bring Ellie inside the barn. For the first few weeks, we tried to get close to Ellie, but the horse chose to walk away from us to the farthest corner of the pasture or to stand in the middle of a huge mud puddle where we wouldn't want to walk. Laura took the horse's standoffish behavior personally. She broke into tears one day when Ellie wouldn't come near her. Laura felt the horse was reacting to her the same way the children and teachers did at school.

In only a short time, Ellie's connection, or lack of it, with Laura had made possible a significant breakthrough. Laura could finally talk about her feelings and grieve for her lack of friendship. As she stood there sobbing, I noticed, out of the corner of my eye, Ellie slowly making her way toward us. I nodded in Ellie's direction so Laura would follow the motion of my head, and said, "We have company." Ellie walked directly between Laura and me and placed her large black head against the distraught girl's chest. She let out the longest sigh when Laura wrapped her arms around the horse's head and began to stroke her ears and mane.

After this powerful encounter, Laura and Ellie easily developed a relationship. Whenever Ellie saw Laura arrive at the stable, the horse would wait for her girlfriend at the pasture gate. During her sessions, Laura was also around other youth her age who were there for riding lessons. She chatted with the other girls and started to enjoy their company.

One day while changing her shoes in the barn, Laura discovered to her embarrassment that she was wearing mismatched socks. "I'm so glad that I'm just here with my horse," she said. "Ellie doesn't care what I look like. All the kids at school would have really given me a hard time." Another rider overheard Laura's comment, pointed down at her own mismatched socks, and said, "I do that all the time. I think the horses like it, because it's colorful for them." We all laughed, and I complimented Laura on how her confidence had grown since she'd started riding lessons. She didn't seem on edge when she was at the barn with her horse. As if to register her agreement, Ellie chimed in with an earsplitting neighing.

Laura and Ellie bonded over their grooming sessions, and these, along with her riding lessons, taught Laura some useful stress-reduction techniques. If she arrived at the barn angry, shut down, or unmotivated, finger-combing Ellie's mane helped her relax and become mindful.

Ellie was a great source of feedback when Laura was moody. The intuitive horse would do things such as walking ahead of Laura, getting into her space, nudging her forward, or resisting going to familiar places. During these times, when Ellie made it clear she needed more structure and Laura's attention, the horse's behavior made it impossible for Laura to stay disengaged or lost in her depressing thoughts. These moments produced some of our most powerful sessions, because I often needed to say very little. Laura's mood would lighten as she attended to her horse, and Ellie would adjust her behavior and become attentive and playful.

Although school remained a challenge for Laura, she slowly recognized that being herself was her greatest strength. It was okay to ask for help if she struggled with a tough task. The small risks she took in learning how to care for and ride Ellie helped her take small risks with her peers. If new situations paralyzed her with fear, Laura would visualize Ellie's soft brown eyes and slow, even breathing. She kept a small piece of Ellie's hair secured in a locket, which she wore around her neck. Whenever she doubted herself, Laura would touch or smell the braid of Ellie's hair and imagine herself riding above all the confusion until it was safe to come back to grazing in a peaceful pasture.

Laura summed up Ellie's influence on her life one day with words I will always remember: "So many times, I thought I was going to fail and everyone at the barn would never talk to me again.

Ellie makes me feel special and she loves me. She is there with me at school and has given me invisible wings."

A Llama Thanks Justin

One of my nonprofit organization's teaching sites is the Children's Country Day School, a six-acre facility nestled in a residential area just outside of Saint Paul. At first glance, this preschool looks like a typical home-based facility, because it has been modified with various additions and resides in a neighborhood setting with similar houses. But when you walk behind the main building, you discover a wonderland of outdoor play areas, gardens, and a menagerie of domestic and farm animals.

Tanya's llama

The school is home to animal species that will pique the interest of almost anyone — a beautiful blond corn snake; two lop-eared rabbits who live in a maze of underground tunnels; Sylvester and Sweet Pea, a bonded pair of chickens; a pony; a mother-daughter pair of donkeys and a pair of miniature horses; a flock of goats; one lone sheep; and a mated pair of llamas with their three young offspring. Curious chickens strut up to greet visitors. Donkeys bray loudly and mournfully.

One spring afternoon, I received a call from a high school interested in performing its annual day of community service by having students work with me at the Children's Country Day School. The care and maintenance of the animals is never-ending at the day school, so it was a perfect site for hosting a group of teenagers ready to work. The high school's staff expressed some concern about one student, "Justin," who was new to the class. He was having great difficulty forming healthy relationships. He did not trust others and was so disruptive that the school, the community, and his family could barely manage him. However, when Justin learned the class was going to a farm and asked if he could join in, it was the first time he took an active interest in a school activity.

After they arrived, I gave the class a safety review and a brief tour. Then I divided the students according to projects. The girls signed up for painting buildings and gardening, while most of the guys opted to help clear buckthorn from the wooded areas. As the groups dispersed, Justin remained and asked to do something with the animals.

"It might involve poop," I said.

"That's okay," he replied.

"Then the llamas would be grateful for your help."

When we entered the paddock, before Justin started the cleanup chores, the youngest llama, a three-year-old female named Mokie, met Justin as her parents kept a watchful eye from their distant dirt mound. "I've never been this close to a llama. Will she spit on me?" Justin whispered.

Mokie easily stood a foot taller than Justin. With much deliberate care and attention, she bent her giraffelike neck down so she could look directly into the boy's eyes. She batted her long eyelashes while chewing her cud and flicked her tufted ears back and forth as if she were trying to get a clearer picture of this being standing before her. I could see Justin had almost stopped breathing. "Can I pet her?" he asked. "If she gives you permission," I said.

Asking permission to do something and honoring a reply to his request were not skills Justin readily exercised. When he cautiously tried to touch Mokie's oversized ears, the llama pulled away, just out of reach. When he stepped forward to try again, she took a step backward. He stepped again, and she backed away. He stepped more quickly the fourth time, and Mokie trotted toward her siblings. The entire family of llamas then walked to the other side of the pasture. Frustrated, Justin stood with his hands on his hips and demanded I show him the tricks to catching llamas.

Justin's teacher, who stood in the paddock with us, must have observed his interaction and focus on the llama. When she joined the discussion Justin and I were having, she said, "Justin, sometimes I feel the same way when I'm with you." Justin gave her a puzzled glare, but she continued. "I really want to help you. I feel like you are that little llama. You move away when others try to support you or give you advice. Because you only move just beyond range, we keep thinking there's hope."

At the teacher's honest words, Justin rolled his eyes and let out a big sigh. Then he grabbed a shovel and wheelbarrow. Maintaining a pensive silence, he began cleaning out the llamas' shed.

Hard work and fresh air can do much to lighten a person's mood. Not long after his teacher gave him a dose of reality, Justin started asking me all sorts of detailed questions about the llamas. He was amazed to learn that llamas prefer to have designated areas for bathroom duties, and he thought Mokie was the most beautiful being he had ever seen. Xena and Dexter, the llama parents, stuck their noses around the corner to observe our poop-scooping chores. They must have given the all-clear signal to their children, because the other three llamas soon joined us. I could see Justin watching them out of the corner of his eye, but he kept his back turned and gave no indication he was interested in them.

As Justin made the final trip to the compost pile, Mokie trailed along after him. He was oblivious to her soft and gentle presence and startled when he turned around to find her standing about ten feet in front of him. I softly coached him to look down instead of directly at her. "Keep your body relaxed. If she approaches, let her show you how comfortable she is before you touch her."

I moved a little closer to Justin and continued to engage him in conversation so he would breathe. This llama family was known for investigating people by sniffing them, something the children called "angel kisses." As Justin continued to look down, Mokie casually walked toward him and smelled the side of his head. He slowly turned in her direction. "Don't touch her yet," I advised.

Justin's lack of reaction was exactly what Mokie needed in order to confidently smell his cheek ever so lightly. Then she moved her nose down to his hand and gave it a gentle bump. I smiled at Justin. When he looked at me with questioning eyes, I nodded. With the same level of tenderness as Mokie's, he touched the llama's shoulder.

Before he left the farm that day, Justin mused, "I bet Mokie was thanking me for getting her bathroom all cleaned out. I'll never forget her."

Justin had arrived that morning a young man who acted up at school and had little social interaction with the rest of his class. As the students boarded the bus, it pleased me to see that he was smiling and sharing stories of the day with two other students. Being befriended by llamas had served him well.

Amanda and Woodstock

Due to some early childhood trauma, twelve-year-old "Amanda" had developed a high level of anxiety early on in her life. Up to this point, school had been a place where she excelled, but now even there Amanda was becoming physically sick when she attended. Unusual fears began to surface, about getting lost or her parents dying. Little by little, Amanda's world shrunk to the confines of her home and the family car, to places within arm's reach of her mother or father.

Because of her fears, the typical AAI session with a dog would not be appropriate for Amanda. In addition, she was allergic to cats, and meeting the horses proved to be overwhelming.

During one session with Amanda I asked, "Would you like to meet Woodstock?" Woodstock stands about ten inches high, weighs about two pounds, and looks like a soft, fuzzy, blond creature out of an animated film — and she's a chicken, a silkie, to be exact.

On a warm, sunny day, Amanda and I sat on a blanket underneath the trees while Woodstock patiently waited in her kennel. Amanda observed her through the metal door and asked, "Are you sure she's a chicken? I've never seen anything like her before."

I had constructed a small area surrounded by a two-foot fence with water and chicken snacks. I placed Woodstock and her kennel inside it, away from the main chicken coop. During our first session with this special bird, Amanda and I observed the chicken, while she asked questions and got comfortable meeting Woodstock.

Each week, we kept to this same routine, but I also added activities to help Amanda become more engaged with Woodstock and responsible for her care. The chickens live in a cooplike

Tanya's Woodstock

structure that resembles a shed. Attached to it is a run enclosed by a chain-link fence, where people can stand and interact with the chickens. Amanda prepared the food and water that went into the entire enclosure, and she helped me set up and clean the pen where Woodstock lived. She also collected eggs and watched how Woodstock behaved with the rest of the flock.

Although reluctant at first to pet a chicken, Amanda gained confidence over the weeks. While I held Woodstock in a basket, Amanda tentatively touched her. We talked about how the basket was Woodstock's safe place, that she liked it because sometimes the rest of the world was scary and chickens needed places where they could hide.

At the farm, chickens usually take dust or dirt baths. However, Woodstock required a soap-and-water bath when she went into the office with me to help with AAI. I decided Amanda would be a perfect assistant for this chore. Her face lit up when I described the adventure ahead. "Can I get her all soapy?" she asked. "You bet," I answered.

The project began with us filling three buckets with warm water. Amanda poured the organic, mild shampoo into one bucket, the vegetable glycerin for conditioner into another bucket, and filled the third bucket with plain water. Giving Woodstock a bath involved putting her into the first bucket with the soap, rinsing her in the second bucket with the glycerin, and then gently placing her in the third bucket for a final rinse in the clear water to remove any product that remained on her body.

Amanda didn't hesitate to help me bathe the very patient chicken. We managed to get equally sloppy by the time Woodstock was clean and wrapped snugly in a towel like a burrito. Thankfully, it was a very warm day with no wind, so we took her outside for a little air-drying and fluffing. I showed Amanda how to gently pick

up and separate Woodstock's feathers all over her body. I noticed a
new intensity and energy in the girl that she hadn't shown before in
our work together. Woodstock purred through the whole encounter, her eyes signaling her dreamy state.

Amanda was scheduled to start a new school so she could
receive more social and emotional support. Her mother wistfully
remarked that she wished Woodstock could come to this new
school. "Well, why not?" I asked.

Over the next few weeks, parents, teachers, Amanda, and I created a special class for Amanda, where she would bring Woodstock
and teach her fellow students all about chickens. Amanda and I
worked on what she was going to say, practiced some of Woodstock's tricks, and decorated a basket for carrying Woodstock to
school.

In her class, I became Amanda's assistant and Woodstock's support. Together, they captured the attention of the entire class as well
as the curiosity of any teacher who passed by the room. At the end
of class, while Amanda stood quietly rocking Woodstock in her
basket, another student approached them and asked, "How do you
know so much about chickens?"

With evident pride, Amanda explained, "I met Woodstock at
this farm, and we got to hang out. She was a lot of fun to train. I
never knew chickens were so smart. But the best part is how she
likes to be with me. She makes me laugh."

To these three special children — Laura, Justin, and Amanda —
and countless others, animals bring a sense of comfort, joy, serenity,
and healing. Animals also alter and normalize institutional pro-
cesses by helping remove the stigma associated with mental health,
special education, and counseling. I have such gratitude for all
the animal partners who deliver lessons in patience, confidence,

determination, and relationships. They act as a portal through which I am able to reach children and offer them hope.

Meditation

During times when you have connected with nature, what did you find in its simplicity and stillness? How have animals linked you with the natural world?

Lille Is an Angel on a Leash

Barbara L. Babikian, SUGAR LOAF, NEW YORK

"Lille, Lille. Is that you, Lille?" I was shopping at an outlet mall near my home one day when I heard someone calling my Shetland sheepdog (Sheltie), Lille. I turned and saw behind her a little boy in a wheelchair. The woman said, "Lille visited my son after he had a heart transplant. Do you know the impact you've had on kids' lives? Or on their parents?"

It is amazing to hear from a parent that you and your dog have brought joy to them in such a short time. Lille comforts the children by letting them pet, hug, and hold her for a few minutes, and something fabulous happens. She has been making children's lives better for years now. Somehow, she always seems to be in the right place at the right time to give children the compassion they need and to ease tough times.

After bringing my eleven-pound, mahogany-sable dog home with me from Michigan as a puppy in June 2000, I wanted to try animal-assisted therapy with her. My older Shelties served in this way and liked it. Since she is a small Sheltie and tinier than my other dogs, I planned to take Lille everywhere with me. But she turned out to be more timid than my other dogs, hiding when someone knocked at the door to our home. Would she be fearful when I put her in the arms of strangers?

I decided to ease Lille into the job of doing animal-assisted therapy by taking her to nursing homes to visit elderly patients, who would be gentle with her. As soon as I placed Lille in bed with a nursing home resident, she moved her body closer to the person, got very relaxed, and fell asleep. She was naturally calm — a necessity at some of the facilities we would be visiting.

I had always wanted to do this type of service with children, but I knew I couldn't think only of what I wanted. I had to discover what kind of work would be best for my dog and me as a team. I hoped Lille would be great with kids, but I didn't know if she had the personality and could develop the skills for working with them.

One day, Lille and I were in a pet supply store when two children, a brother and sister, began following us around, wanting to pet Lille. Their mother said, "Leave the puppy alone." I assured her, "Don't worry. Lille is a therapy dog. I would like to have her work with children someday."

The little boy took off his baseball cap, revealing that he was bald. Only seven years old, he had a horseshoe-shaped scar around his head that marked where he had had surgery. His mother said, "There's a program at the children's hospital where my son was treated. It is called Angel on a Leash. You should contact them." She explained that Angel on a Leash is a nonprofit organization, headquartered in New York, that provides and monitors highly trained teams of insured volunteer handlers and their dogs for animal-assisted therapy at health-care facilities across the country. I immediately liked the idea of contacting the organization.

Lille Prepares for Her New Calling

I called Angel on a Leash and spoke with Greer Griffith, the director of programs. She explained that Lille had to be at least a year old and registered with the Delta Society in order to qualify for training with Angel on a Leash. The Delta Society is a national nonprofit organization formed in 1977 to provide training and testing for people who want to do animal-assisted therapy. Since we were already registered with the Delta Society, we set up a meeting with Greer so she could evaluate Lille.

Greer needed to determine if Lille had the temperament for the sensitive task of visiting children in a hospital. After Greer's assessment, we were ready to volunteer with Angel on a Leash. We now had to meet the requirements of the children's hospital. I took an orientation class, which explained the hospital rules, regulations, and policies pertaining to animal-assisted-therapy teams. Twice I took a PPD (purified protein derivative) test, which determines whether a person has developed an immune response to the bacterium that causes tuberculosis. I had to be fingerprinted, and both Lille and I were photographed for our hospital badges. We were then ready to go; Greer would shadow us on our first couple of visits.

Lille and Chloe

We established a routine to prepare Lille each time for her important work. Twenty-four hours before the therapy visit, I would give her a bath and make sure her nails were trimmed. When we were ready to leave for the hospital, I'd grab her bag, which contained her Delta Society vest and ID, which expires every two years, her health record, our hospital badges, pictures of Lille for the children to keep, a brush, an extra leash, a water bowl, and a few other things dogs need. In the car, I would secure Lille in her doggy car seat and put her seat belt on for the hour-long drive to New York City. After we arrived at the hospital, I'd put her therapy dog vest on, and she would pull me toward the entrance doors, eager to start work.

At the hospital we would pick up the approved list of twenty to forty children who were waiting for a visit from the therapy dogs on four different floors. Before entering a patient's room, I'd check outside the door to make sure we were allowed to enter. Sometimes there were special instructions saying, for example, that visitors must wear gloves and a gown, or that the child was not allowed to have visitors — information that might contradict the approved list of children because of the constant flux of patients leaving and new ones arriving. Once I saw that it was okay to enter, I'd knock on the door and ask, "Would you like to meet a therapy dog?"

Denice Makes a Faithful Friend

Twelve-year-old "Denice" was one of the children on my list during a visit to the children's hospital. When Lille and I walked into Denice's hospital room and I asked if she would like us to visit, she grinned and said yes.

After we entered the room, where her mother and grand-mother were visiting, I asked Denice if there were any sensitive areas or tubes I should be aware of. She told me she'd just had surgery on her leg, and it would be best if I placed Lille on the side that had not been operated on. As I laid Lille next to her, I said, "Cuddle up." As is her style, tiny Lille repositioned her body several times until she was pressed up against Denice. Lille then settled into a nice cuddle and fell asleep.

After we had stayed with Denice for a while, it was time to visit the next child on my list. As usual, I was careful to say good-bye and not say, "See you soon." I left Denice's room thinking I would never see her again.

About a year later, I was leaving a child's room with Lille and was surprised to see Denice's mother running out of a room toward me. She explained that her daughter was back in the hospital for a second leg surgery. She was in a lot of pain after the second operation and had just said to her, "The only thing I need now is Lille by my side."

As Lille and I followed Denice's mother back to the teenager's room, I knew I had to be strong and not allow my tears to flow. I felt joyful that after only meeting her once, Denice had remembered Lille. Lille had touched the heart of this twelve-year-old girl and eased her anxiety on their first visit. Now she would do it again. Our visit with Denice that day was a happy reunion.

Years later, I was heading home from a facility with my new therapy dog, Dusty, another Sheltie. I needed to make a quick stop at a store, so I put Dusty's vest on him. The owners knew Dusty and the work he did, so they didn't mind him coming into the store with me. I placed a blanket in the bottom of my cart and put Dusty in the cart. A woman came up to me and commented on Dusty's therapy dog vest. Then she looked at me quizzically and said, "I think you visited my child with your dog when she was in the hospital."

At last, I recognized the woman as Denice's mother. I answered, "Yes, but this is not Lille." She touched my arm and, with tears in her eyes, said, "You do not know what those visits meant to my daughter. After Denice's last stay in the hospital, she got a dog when she came home."

The girl had ultimately needed one surgery on each leg. All her life, she had dreaded the inevitable painful surgeries she would one day have. On the difficult days following those surgeries, Lille had lain by her side and comforted her. Her compassion had helped Denice forget for a moment that she was in a hospital.

The timing of Lille's visits to the child had been remarkable. After being there for Denice's first hospitalization, it was not likely that Lille would be there for the second surgery, given that she does therapy work at the children's hospital only two Sundays a month. And what were the odds that I would encounter Denice's grateful mother in this particular store years after her daughter's ordeal had ended? I live a little more than an hour's drive from the hospital. Neither of us knew we lived in the same town, and we had not been in contact other than for those two visits with Denice. Yet she had recognized me and was able to express appreciation for the difference Lille's visits had made.

Lille Goes Where She's Needed

Another time when we walked into the hospital, one of the staff said there was a specific child Lille needed to see. "Joshua," an eight-year-old boy, had suddenly stopped moving because of a neurological problem. After Lille and I found Joshua's room, I asked his mother for permission to place Lille in the child's arms so that we wouldn't displace any tubes. She picked up her son's hand and stroked Lille with it, trying unsuccessfully to get the child to move his fingers or arm. "See how soft Lille is," the mother whispered.

After about fifteen minutes, the nurse came in to care for the boy. When I tried to take Lille out from under his arm, he tightened it around her and would not let go. Then the boy wiggled his fingers for the first time since the neurological problem had started, about thirty days earlier. At that moment, I could not take Lille from Joshua. The nurse said, "I'll come back."

The nurse returned later, and I had to do something I always dread — take Lille away from a child who is having a successful visit with her. Joshua needed medical attention, so I did what I had to do. While Joshua screamed for Lille, I had to draw upon my emotional strength to remove my little dog from his grasp.

As I walked around the curtain to leave the room, Joshua's mother came away from her son's bedside to talk to me in private. She didn't want to cry in front of her son — like many of these mothers, she found the strength to hide her emotions from her sick child. But beyond the curtain, out of Joshua's view, she grabbed my hand and, with tears running down her cheeks, said, "Thank you." Lille had brought hope into the lives of one more suffering child and his worried parent.

Lille Expands Her Service

I had always wanted to volunteer at the Ronald McDonald House in New York City. Ronald McDonald House New York provides a temporary home-away-from-home for pediatric cancer patients and their families. After a special event where I met a child who was staying there, I decided it was time to join the Ronald McDonald House team.

One day, Lille was relaxing for about fifteen minutes with a seven-year-old boy who was at the Ronald McDonald House for a second time while undergoing treatment. First Lille closed her eyes, and then the boy closed his eyes. They were obviously enjoying each other's company. When the boy got up to do something else, his mother came over to me and asked, "Do you think Lille would lie down by me?"

I knew this boy's mother was in pain too, and that Lille would give her the comfort she needed. I placed my dog by the woman's belly. This is the way I had taught Lille to nestle near me while we watch TV. I said, "Cuddle up, Lille." She moved until she was snuggled close to the woman. After about twenty minutes the mother got up, came over to me, and whispered in my ear, "You do not know how much I needed her. Thank you."

I also run the Angel on a Leash therapy dog program as the coordinator of animal-assisted interactions at New Alternatives for Children in New York City, which provides support for birth, foster, and adoptive families who care at home for children with special medical needs. Since 1982, the organization has served New York

City's most vulnerable children, those who are medically fragile, poor, abused, and/or neglected. New Alternatives for Children provides a continuum of health and social services primarily for children and their families who live in poverty. The organization seeks to enable them to remain in, or return to, their homes whenever possible, or to be adopted by loving families when necessary. Its philosophy is that all children, including those who are chronically ill or physically challenged, deserve a safe, loving home and a bright future.

Lille and I visit New Alternatives for Children once a week. Girls, and then boys, come to the facility on alternate weeks — five girls one week, and four boys the next week — specifically for my animal-assisted therapy interactions program on Thursdays from 5:00 to 6:30 PM. New Alternatives for Children sends a van to pick up the children and bring them to the organization's office for my program. Many of the children have never had a dog or even petted one. Some are fearful of Lille at first, but she soothes them and helps them overcome their fears. With her help I teach the children that dogs should be treated with kindness, and we show them what unconditional love means.

Off-Duty Lille

I have a total of three Shelties and one German shepherd. My older Sheltie and the German shepherd didn't want anything to do with Lille, so I decided to get Dusty for her as a puppy playmate. When Lille is working or is somewhere else outside our home, she is very serious and always on her best behavior. But off duty, she and Dusty play nonstop in the house and yard, and she gets to enjoy life as a regular dog. Shelties are known to be barkers and herders. Lille is definitely a Sheltie, barking and chasing deer off our property and into the woods.

Lille turned five years old in March 2011 and has many years left for touching lives. As for me, I wish we could visit children every day. Each time Lille meets a child in need, magic happens. I am honored to witness the miracles.

Meditation

Has an animal made magic happen for you or a child you know? Have you ever considered training to volunteer for animal-assisted therapy?

Missy's Magical Llamas

Mona J. Sams, TROUTVILLE, VIRGINIA

Megan has already eaten breakfast but is not in the right mood for going to work this morning. She would rather stand around, soaking sun into her skin and gazing off into a cloudless sky. Is she only being stubborn, or does she really need a break? I watch her shuffling her feet and looking tired. Megan is getting older and has always been great on the job. I decide to give her a pat on the back and the day off. Her younger friend is eager for the opportunity to work and follows me to the gate.

It may appear from this incident that Megan is a senior citizen nearing retirement. She is. But she's also a llama. Her coworker is our youngest llama, Munchkin, a fellow full of personality who wants to work every day. At my farm, llamas aren't only fascinating to look at. They are staff.

I'm a licensed occupational therapist, and I incorporate animals into my treatment approach to children with autism, post–traumatic stress disorder, cerebral palsy, and visual and hearing impairments. The animals I work with serve as catalysts for interaction with my clients. To my knowledge, I am the only occupational therapist who transports llamas and alpacas in order to have their help in treating children with autism and post–traumatic stress disorder.

I especially love working with llamas and children. Llamas are extraordinarily adaptable. I call them "land dolphins" because of their intuitiveness and sensitivity to humans. Since mature llamas weigh from 280 to 400 pounds, they are much lighter than horses, which makes them easier to transport and less intimidating for children.

Llamas have a split toe, which makes them light-footed. If a llama accidentally steps on a child's foot, there is less chance of injury than if a horse were to do the same. And when horses become frightened, they tend to run away. Llamas, when confronted by problems, figure out how to solve them. For example, if a wheelchair rolls in front of a llama, the animal will move to the side to avoid a collision, rather than rear up. And it's a big plus that, if a child weighs less than a hundred pounds, he or she can ride a llama. A llama can carry one-third to one-quarter of his or her weight.

Because they are communal poopers, I never have to worry about accidental poops when I move my llamas to new locations. All I have to do is bring along a bucket of their poop (I know, it sounds gross!), put it down in one spot, and let the llamas smell it. The scent signals that it's okay for them to poop there, and they won't go anywhere else. I have been able to ride with a llama in an elevator to the second floor of a building, and even been filmed for television programs, without having any mess to clean up.

Several of the llamas like spending time inside buildings so much that they don't want to leave. Then they do what is called kushing — they sit down and tuck their four legs underneath them and refuse to move. When llamas sleep, they get into the kushing position and lay their necks and heads between their front legs. While kushing when awake, they can pop their heads straight up. When this happens indoors, our clients get to sit on chairs beside the llamas, and the llamas rest their necks and heads on the clients' laps. The clients consider it a special experience. Afterward, I have to use a little bribery to entice the llamas to leave, but the clients really enjoy it when the llamas act like difficult teenagers.

It's another plus that llamas are hypoallergenic, so not many people have problems being around them. Llamas are beautiful creatures, majestic and easy to lead, and their fur makes a gorgeous fiber. Children love touching, petting, and hugging them. Llamas, who are polite and accommodating by nature, are extremely receptive to people with special needs. If a child can't reach a llama's head, the animal will lower it for petting. I am continually amazed at how compassionate llamas are.

Missy and Her Magical Llamas

One of my many satisfying animal-assisted therapy experiences has been with an amazing survivor named "Missy." She and her five siblings were removed from their family of origin when Missy was about five years old. The severe abuse they suffered was horrific and occurred on every level. Missy was sent to one foster home temporarily and then relocated to her present home, where she and her older brother were adopted.

Missy became my client when she was twelve years old, after her adoptive family began being serviced by a program at a local medical center. Missy suffered from post–traumatic stress disorder and was visually impaired. A quiet and polite child, she wore thick glasses as a result of macular degeneration. She was having a terrible time at school, where the children were cruel to her. (Fortunately she now attends a private school and is having a much more positive experience.)

Buckwheat, a baby llama, was the first animal whom shy Missy met when I brought Buckwheat and her mother, Vanilla Bean, to the medical center from my farm in Troutville. "He's so adorable and sweet," she said. Then I introduced her to Dixie, a Great Dane; Squeaker, a Jack Russell terrier; and Izzy, a briard puppy. Missy was enchanted by the animals and excited about a return visit. On her second visit to the treatment center, she was thrilled to ride Megan, my oldest therapy llama. Missy came to the treatment center every week after that and was able to watch Buckwheat grow into adulthood.

Missy especially liked grooming and bathing the llamas. She also learned how to card the llama fiber we save each year after shearing, and this activity built strength in her arms. And she became good at felting and using fiber for art projects. Missy loved leading llamas through obstacle courses. She grew in confidence and calmly and patiently trained llamas to enter the Llama Fest shows that we host for children with special needs. At our Llama Fest, clients compete in their individual categories according to age and skill and win placement ribbons and trophies.

The medical center that had funded Missy's visits ended the program after her fifth visit to the center. She

Missy and Mona's llama Andy

was heartbroken and thought she might never see the animals or me again. About that time, I opened my private clinic, and she became one of my first clients.

Missy grew so proficient and confident that when I had to go out of town, she and her family would go to the farm and take care of the animals. I asked Missy to write about her experiences of filling in for me at the farm. She wrote:

The llamas sometimes spit on each other during feeding time. My mom does not like to be spit on, so I have to do most of the feeding. My brother helps sometimes to get the llamas in the correct fence while I carry their feed. Munchkin, a little llama, loves to follow me around during feeding. I always give him special attention.

After I feed the llamas I help my mom with the rabbits. My favorite is Little Foot, because he's small and cuddly. My family works as a team to make sure the sheep, llamas, goats, rabbits, and dogs are all well cared for. We love going to the farm to help Mona and the animals. The only time it is hard is when it is cold or dark.

Missy loves to draw, and she makes beautiful fiber projects, which we display on the clinic's walls. Sometimes her projects are sold at a local boutique. She designed a brochure for one of our Llama Fests that featured a llama eating a sunflower, and we had T-shirts made with her design to sell at the event.

When Missy's family got a border collie, the girl began training the dog herself. She has given him agility training and taught him to play flyball. Now, at the age of seventeen, she has joined a group of flyball enthusiasts who provide her with a social life beyond that of her friends at school. Eventually Missy will have a service dog because of her impaired night vision. Meanwhile, she has gained so much self-confidence that she decided to make a contribution to the clinic by helping me with other clients who have disabilities. She is very patient with children with special needs and always willing to help them.

The young girl with severe post–traumatic stress disorder, whose bad nightmares and lack of confidence made her withdraw from the world, has transformed into a bright and confident young woman who will go to college, just as her older brother did. I was thrilled when Missy offered to serve on the board of directors of our nonprofit organization.

Best to let Missy share the conclusion of her journey:

Working with the animals has taught me to be independent and sure of myself. Working with the llamas' fiber sparked my interest in art. With Mona's help, I have become an artist.

Through animal-assisted therapy, I found out that animals have needs and feelings too. While learning about the animals, I learned about myself. I know now that I can help others overcome bad experiences. I can still be a good person even though bad things have happened to me.

Sometimes Missy will come to the clinic after a stressful week at school, and she won't want to work on a fiber project. At these times, she might relax with the animals, take new bunnies out to run on the lawn, do obstacle training with a rabbit, train one of the Jack Russells, walk with or lead one of the llamas, or just play. This young woman missed a whole chunk of her childhood, and whatever she wants to do here is okay with me and the animals. And don't we all grow and learn better when doing something we love, with creatures who love us back?

Meditation

Who would have thought llamas would be so good at healing children? What are the unlikely sources of healing in your life?

Simon, My Cat with Special Needs, Gives Hope to Children

Diana Richett, LAKEWOOD, COLORADO

As I work in the kitchen, I feel a nudge against my ankle. I know without looking down that my eight-pound, eight-year-old cat Simon is trying to get my attention. I extend my hand down, and he nestles his head in my palm and purrs. He massages my hand with his silken black head.

I walk into the family room, and he follows, pulling himself with his front legs while dragging his lower body. His back legs crisscross as they move back and forth with each step of his front legs. While I sit on the couch, Simon looks up at me, blinking his gorgeous green eyes. He smiles by showing the tip of his tongue and his upper teeth. He clearly is asking to be picked up and seated on the couch next to me. When I look at Simon, I do not mind his misshapen body. I only hope that I have this beloved, little, domestic shorthaired cat for at least another eight years.

At the time I adopted Simon, I was a volunteer at an animal shelter and participated in its humane education program, which teaches children respect and compassion for all living creatures and shows them how to take care of companion animals. Simon was good-natured and friendly with people, so I decided to incorporate him into the presentations. At the age of ten months, and for the next couple of years, he went with me to schools, residential treatment centers, and the Lookout Mountain Youth Services Center, an institution for juvenile offenders. Definitely actor material, Simon knew how to work a room. Children's initial sadness and concern for the "crippled kitty" soon turned to smiles as they tried to get the attention of this charming cat.

One year, with Christmas presents in tow, I brought Simon to visit a class of third graders at Molholm Elementary School in Lakewood, Colorado. Many of the children at this school live in poverty, and one out of every ten of the students is homeless. The teacher of this class helps her students and their families through her nonprofit food bank.

When we entered the class, the children were delighted to see the Christmas presents. They quickly circled the cat carrier and seated themselves on the floor around Simon and me. Some of them tried to squeeze in to sit closer to Simon. They listened intently as I told Simon's story. All of them wanted to pet him before we distributed presents. Simon and I later received notes of thanks addressed to "Santa's Little Helper" from the children, along with crayon drawings of him. A couple of children expressed hope that Simon would get better, while others described him as cute, pretty, and very special. One little girl said, "I love your cat as much as I love my baby brother." Many asked if I would bring Simon back to see them again.

Simon's Remarkable Journey

It has been a remarkable journey for Simon since August 2002, when I was blessed by this very special addition to my family. At that time, he was a tiny, three-month-old kitten. Although I am a practicing attorney representing children, I am also a certified veterinary technician. My medical knowledge made it possible for me to adopt and care for animals with special needs, including cats with diabetes, lymphoma, hyperthyroidism, chronic respiratory issues, and radial hypoplasia, or twisted front limbs. But none of my animals ever had needs as complex as Simon's. Born with severe spinal deformities, he had pectus excavatum, or funnel chest, a skeletal deformity of the chest characterized by a depressed sternum, as well as kyphosis, an abnormal curvature of the thoracic spine. His hind legs, which were paralyzed, were also contorted and looked as if they were on backward.

Simon couldn't urinate on his own, and as I fumbled while learning to express his bladder three times a day, he proved to be very good-natured and patient with me. In spite of all his physical issues, he quickly acquired the run of the house and pulled himself around, dragging his back legs behind him.

At age four, Simon was diagnosed with hypertrophic cardiomyopathy, or an enlarged heart, which can result in congestive heart failure and death. After repeated ultrasounds and specialized blood tests, his diagnosis was changed, for the better, to cor pulmonale, or right-sided heart enlargement due to pulmonary problems. He also was diagnosed with asthma, which required a daily medication regime that included two puffs from an inhaler. He learned to take pills without a struggle and also accepted the inhaler. When I asked his cardiologist, "How long do you think Simon will live?" the doctor replied, "He shouldn't even be here."

It's true that Simon has defied the odds. No one knows how he managed to survive outdoors until he was three or four weeks old. A man found him under a trash Dumpster in Rifle, Colorado. He called the Friends of Rifle Animal Shelter. Seeing the crippled kitten with what appeared to be a broken back, and possibly thinking he should put him out of his misery, the man asked Melody, the shelter volunteer, "What do you want me to do with him? Do you want me to stomp on him?"

Of course, Melody told him no and asked the man to bring the kitten to the shelter. The staff immediately rushed Simon to a veterinary clinic. Seeing the condition of this kitten, the veterinarian could easily have opted to euthanize Simon, but she decided to give him a chance. The clinic's veterinary technician, Cindy, fostered the kitten until he was ready to be adopted.

With his amazing spirit and happy attitude, Simon touched the hearts of his friends in Rifle. But it would be a daunting task to find a home for such a kitty with special needs. The shelter enlisted the help of Best Friends Animal Society, and its staff suggested placing Simon on the Pets with Disabilities website, where I found a description of him.

A few months earlier, I had lost my beloved and special pit bull, Quincy. Although initially looking to adopt a disabled dog, I researched Simon's contact information and found that he was in a small shelter in Colorado, almost two hundred miles west of Denver. Soon, Simon came home with me and moved on to a life in which he would bring joy, comfort, and hope to the lives of many children.

Simon Becomes a Therapy Cat

In the summer of 2009, Simon and I became a registered therapy team with the American Humane Association Animal-Assisted Therapy (AAT) program. Founded in 2001 by Diana McQuarrie, the American Humane Association AAT strives to build healthy, humane communities by enhancing people's lives with the human-animal bond through animal-assisted activities and therapy. Last year, the American Humane Association AAT worked in acute and long-term care facilities, hospitals, hospices, mental health centers, group homes and residential treatment centers, homeless shelters, schools, and libraries. Volunteer teams served more than fifty facilities and improved the lives of more than 125,000 people.

As part of this program, Simon and I tutor children at Denver's Westwood Opportunity Center, through the University of Denver's

Bridge Project. The program provides after-school education for children in public housing neighborhoods. Our mission is to help these children graduate from high school and go on to college or learn a trade.

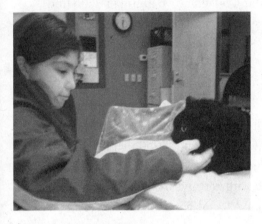

Clara and Diana's Simon

As Simon and I arrive for tutoring, we walk past red brick row homes in the housing project. We immediately hear children's voices. The place bustles with activity. The Bridge Project staff and volunteers help children who range in age from six to eighteen do homework, read stories, and play games; the staff also provides snacks. Simon and I enter the library, which is stocked with many books, games, and school supplies. We sit at a table while we wait for Clara to arrive.

Clara, a pretty Hispanic American child with long dark-brown hair and brown eyes, is ten years old. Simon and I met Clara in September 2009, when she was in the third grade and turning nine years old. We help Clara with homework, particularly mathematics, which includes problems in addition, subtraction, multiplication, division, telling time, measuring, and counting money. We also read a story during each session and sometimes play a game.

Although Clara smiles easily, she was initially shy and reserved with Simon and me. Soon, though, with Simon's encouragement, she opened up more and more. She clearly loved animals. Her voice shaking, she told us about her dog, whom she rescued before a group of teenagers could shoot him in her yard. Then somberly she talked about her aunt's cat, who was cruelly killed, and wondered why people were so mean. A kindhearted child, Clara spoke of her aspirations to be an animal cop and rescue animals from cruelty and neglect. She also said she would like to be a lawyer so she could help people.

As Clara and I built our relationship, Simon became the link in that connection. Clara looked forward to seeing him each week. Simon turned into her companion while I helped with homework. She loved to pet him and liked that Simon listened when she read.

One day, Clara came to the tutoring session in tears, and I could not get her to tell me what upset her. At a loss for how to comfort her, I turned to Simon for help. Speaking to my cat, I said, with Clara listening, "It makes you sad too, Simon, to see Clara so sad. You wish you could do something to make her feel better. Do you think that maybe if she petted you, she would feel better?" While I never did find out what had hurt Clara, by the end of the session she was laughing and obviously feeling a lot happier.

Simon has a special place in my heart and is an integral part of all that is important in my life. He obviously has a purpose in this world that is not defined by his limitations. This cat's amazing spirit and incredible attitude cause people to listen to their hearts, open their minds, and realize that a will to achieve knows no bounds. Simon has done much more than survive. He enriches my life and the lives of every child he meets.

Meditation

Simon's life and ability to bring healing to children aren't thwarted by his limitations. Are there obstacles between you and all you were meant to be that you accept as insurmountable?

Childhood Horses Saved My Life

Nanci Falley, LOCKHART, TEXAS

All my life I had asked for a horse. For birthdays, Christmas, or any gift-giving occasion, a horse was at the top of my wish list. As a sign of my passion for all things equine, my first spoken word was *caballo*, which is Spanish for "horse." Finally, for my tenth birthday, I received my first horse. Molly was a mare of indeterminate age — twenty-two to twenty-five years old. She stood 14.2 hands tall and had a white body marked with large black spots in a tobiano pattern. I loved her with all my heart.

Molly meant so much to me partly because my parents were alcoholics. Even as a child, I took on the burden of protecting my younger brother from the harsh reality of their addiction. I could not rely on my parents to make good decisions for their children. Although my brother found his place in school with friends and never seemed as bothered as I was by our parents' alcoholism, I still tried to keep him from its effects. Because of her loving nature, Molly gave me the joy, love, and opportunity to play that I had missed during the early years of my childhood. She was my rock, and I felt more secure with her than I had in years.

There were no riding instructors in our small south Texas town, so I was self- and Molly-taught. Although a firm teacher, she had a lot of patience for a youngster who had never ridden a horse. When I was learning to mount, however, I inadvertently poked her in the side with the toe of my boot. She started cow-kicking, bringing one hind leg off the ground and kicking sideways at me. I mounted correctly and never again toed her or any other horse. Molly was also a good pony horse, like the mature horses on racetracks who lead younger horses from the paddocks to the track. She never argued about leading another horse as long as I was in her saddle. After I acquired a total of three horses, including Molly, I took Molly for after-school rides, with Molly and me ambling along in the lead and my other two horses walking behind us.

My family was wealthy, so keeping Molly was not a problem. Since neither of my parents was into horses, and both must have wondered how I came to be so completely fascinated by them, they mostly stayed out of the way and let me be on my own with Molly.

By the time I was an energetic tween, I thought I had learned all Molly could teach me. I wanted a younger horse who would be more of a challenge, one I could train from scratch. The opportunity presented itself when Molly and I were on a ride south of our town. A yearling bay filly, who was staked out at the side of the road, broke her tether when she saw us and followed us home. I begged my dad to let me keep her, but he said we had to return the horse. "But Daddy, she picked me," I pleaded. So he called the horse's owners and got her from them for me.

When I was fourteen, I still struggled to cope with my parents' alcoholism and shield my little brother from it. I understood that I couldn't function as an adult and take care of my brother, that I had to stay in school. I became convinced that the only way to cope with my situation was to commit suicide. To my confused mind, this final act promised an end to my having to deal with the negative aspects of my life. That was when the horses' healing magic gave me something to live for. When I was the most suicidal, at age fifteen, the horses' peaceful presence and trusting natures kept me sane and distracted me from thoughts of killing myself.

I rode a lot when I was not in school. I slept in the stable with the horses as often as I could get away with it. My brother, who more readily accepted my parents' behavior and was not interested in animals, started calling me his favorite nickname, Old Horseface. I didn't mind at all; I took it as a compliment.

Slowly but surely the horses helped me to overcome the self-destructive thoughts that plagued me. My horses gave me a reason to get up each morning and to look forward to the day ahead instead of brooding about what my parents might spring on us. I learned to care for the horses to the best of my ability, and I read every training and equine health book I could find.

During my teenage years, an idea began to form in my mind and heart. Horses had saved my life, and I wanted to give to all animals, especially horses, the same level of compassion that my horses had so freely given to me. A life without fear or pain is something every being on earth deserves. I intended to do my best to see that any hurting horse, or any other animal in need, who came across my path would have a quality life.

Nanci's Molly

This may have been a daunting task for anyone less motivated, but I was passionate about it. According to many of my friends and relatives, horses were too expensive and required too much hard work. Their objections went on and on. I ignored all the supposedly good advice of people who urged me not to devote my life to the care of horses and to animal rescue.

But I was determined. As an adult, I now own the Rancho San Francisco farm, named for Saint Francis, patron saint of animals.

I've rescued abandoned and abused horses, donkeys, cats, dogs, potbellied pigs, geese, ducks, chickens, and one peacock. My rescue efforts continue, and I hope they will as long as I draw breath. My most recent rescue is a tiny opossum I found in my yard as an abandoned baby. After ten days of intensive care, she is recovering nicely.

I know this life I am living now, at age seventy-two, would never have been possible without the help of my first equine friends. They and their kind have given me much more than I could ever hope to give them.

Meditation

Has a horse given you the way out of a desperate situation? How have animals from your childhood inspired your choices in life?

Casper the Rabbit Touched My Son

Miriam Palevsky, SOUTH EUCLID, OHIO

My husband, Marvin, and I have been foster parents to more than thirty children, and Michael was one of those children. The three-and-a-half-month-old baby had been severely neglected and perpetually left alone in a crib. Because he had constantly lain face up, his back had become flat and the back of his head was flat and completely bald. (The baldness on the back of his head disappeared, as he eventually grew curly blond hair.)

He would cry at the slightest touch. He couldn't even tolerate someone holding him while feeding him a bottle. When no one touched Michael, he never cried.

At one point the boy became sick with a high fever. Because he was not well enough to scream, we were able, for the first time, to get him used to being held in loving arms. For days, we took turns, never putting him back in his crib. After getting used to our touch during his illness, he became more comfortable with being held. This enabled him to go through the important developmental stage of learning to turn his head from side to side while resting against someone's shoulder.

Other ways in which Michael's development had obviously been delayed included being small for his age, though he was not underweight, and being strangely content to sit and do nothing.

When Michael was seven months old, we noticed that he would make no eye contact with us and couldn't hold his own bottle. He couldn't roll over until he was thirteen months old. If he sat by himself, he didn't reach for things, and he never babbled or attempted speech or other sounds. Because of his severe early neglect, Michael had attachment issues and did not bond with people. He always wanted somebody to be in the room with him, but he didn't care who it was.

Our pediatrician gave us the phone number for our county's early intervention specialists, and we sought help for Michael. Specialists in early childhood development came to our home to assess the boy. We had already raised so many children that it was obvious to us that Michael was experiencing delayed development, but the specialists' evaluations confirmed our suspicions and that of our pediatrician. Michael did not measure up to other children his age. Later, our pediatrician diagnosed his cerebral palsy. A neurologist who examined Michael and read the reports from the intervention team diagnosed him as autistic. When he was one and a half years old, we started taking him to United Cerebral Palsy for therapy three times a week.

About the same time that we began fostering Michael, I became interested in rescuing and learning about rabbits. Previously, I had brought home a rabbit named Peter. For the first year, Peter had sat in a cage, getting very little attention. One day, I bought a book about rabbits and learned everything I was doing wrong and how to care for rabbits properly. I immediately bought Peter a new and much larger cage and put it on the floor so he could go in and out on his own and play. I also got him a litter box and toys. After I verified that he was a boy, I called the veterinarian to get Peter neutered.

Once I had made the improvements in his living conditions, Peter amazed me by turning into a wonderful family pet, and this inspired me to adopt a few new bunnies. The first two I got from a breeder because I was looking for a certain type of rabbit. I then learned that this is a really bad thing to do, because so many rabbits need to be rescued. Petbunny, a group I found on the Internet, taught me more about rabbits, and eventually I got involved in rescuing rabbits and helping them find new and caring homes. All the rabbits we brought home after the first two were from rabbit rescue organizations.

To my surprise, Michael, who could not relate to any human, loved the rabbits we brought into our home, and the rabbits loved him. He would sit with rabbits in his lap and pet them. They nuzzled him, and he returned their affection by hugging, holding, and kissing them. His face would light up whenever he saw them, a reaction he never had with people.

Playing with the rabbits helped bring Michael out of his shell. And we began to notice that the bunnies who couldn't tolerate other people touching them would accept him. Typically children at one or two years of age do not know how to hold a rabbit properly, so bunnies are not the best pets for toddlers. But our rabbits didn't fight with Michael when he picked them up around their bellies and put them in his lap. He would lay his head on them and kiss them. Sometimes he would sit or lie next to the rabbits with his arm around them. Although his fine motor skills were very poor, he never dropped a rabbit, so they trusted him.

Michael's Special Rabbit Friend

One day, we got a message from Michigan Rabbit Rescue telling us that they were looking for a new home for Daisy, an all-white, long-haired English Angora rabbit. Normally English Angoras have a tuft of fur that hangs from their ears, and they are adorable. A rabbit of this breed generally weighs between seven and eight pounds, but Daisy was small, weighing only four pounds.

The unfortunate rabbit was a child's 4-H project gone wrong. The family had kept Daisy in an outdoor hutch that wasn't tall enough to permit her ears to stand up straight. The tufts of fur that naturally hang from an English Angora's ears over the rabbit's forehead instead covered Daisy's eyes, because her ears had lain flopped over for so long in the small hutch. She had been delivered to the rescue group filthy, covered in poop.

I was already planning to drive to Michigan to pick up another rabbit, so I called the group back and said that, on my way back, I would meet one of the group's volunteers in Toledo, Ohio, where Daisy lived, and pick up the rabbit there.

When a volunteer had cleaned her up and cut all the mats out of her fur, it became apparent that Daisy was a male. So Daisy was renamed Poodle because of his long fluffy hair and floppy ears. I thought the rabbit was incredibly cute and very sweet. One of our children suggested we name him Casper. My husband and I decided that would be perfect, because we like the character Casper, the friendly ghost, and this bunny was snowy white.

Michael, who was two by then, and Casper loved each other from the start and wanted to be together constantly. Casper would jump to the edge of the mattress and pull himself up until he could climb through the slats and get inside Michael's crib.

Miriam's Casper

Then he would sleep beside Michael, with the boy's arm wrapped around him. The bunny looked like a plush toy lying motionlessly under Michael's arm. When Casper would awaken, he would not squirm or leave Michael's side as long as the boy slept.

Because Michael's development was delayed, he could do very little, not even communicate. But while he couldn't talk or gesture, his little face could still light up when the rabbit hopped over to him. He'd pick up Casper and sit with and sleep with him. The bunny would follow Michael around the house as if there were no place on earth he would rather be.

One morning when Michael was three, I was in the bathroom getting ready for work, and as I stepped out, I found him standing outside the bathroom door. Unexpectedly, he reached his arms

Matthew and Casper

out and hugged me for the first time. He held me in his embrace for a long while, and I went to work that morning with tears in my eyes, thinking that Michael was finally attached to me. I couldn't let him leave us, now that he was legally available. My husband and I made the decision to adopt him, and we changed his name from Michael to Matthew.

Now we had a boy and a bunny who had both had a rough start in life, found a new and loving home with us, and received new names. With Casper's help, Matthew, at three and a half, finally started to speak.

Life Changes

Unfortunately, some of my bunnies became ill from mycotoxin poisoning caused by infected rabbit food. We spent thousands of dollars trying to get the rabbits well, and a few of those who were sick recovered after extensive treatment. Casper was one of the bunnies who did not get sick.

When Matthew was six, my health deteriorated badly. I had been employed by the same company for eighteen and a half years, but now had to stop working and go on permanent disability. During the next six years I underwent ten surgeries, and, in 2005, I lost the ability to drive and do other everyday activities. We had to stop fostering children and end our rabbit rescue work, because it was financially impossible to tend to the rabbits and keep up with their veterinary care while paying my medical bills.

No longer able to keep the rabbits who had survived the mycotoxin poisoning, I was faced with the sad task of finding new homes for them. Well-cared-for indoor rabbits can live twelve years or more, so although we were grateful to have had Casper as a member of our family for several years, we were faced with the sad task of finding a new home for him too. Michigan Rabbit Rescue and another rabbit rescue group took some of the rabbits.

A woman I used to work with let me know that she had a bunny who'd lost her mate and was very lonely. The woman offered to adopt Casper, and when he and the woman's bunny met, the two white rabbits immediately got along. Soon the two bunnies became a happily bonded pair. The loving family keeps us updated with pictures of Casper, and we are always assured that he is well cared for and cherished.

By the time Casper left us, Matthew was starting to become more communicative. We were going to therapy three days a week, and finally, at age six, he began interacting with people. He continued to improve year after year. As Matthew's ability to love and be loved by other people blossomed, it was as if Casper's important service to my son had been completed. In the past two years, Matthew has been invited to friends' homes for the first time, and he sometimes invites his friends to our house. Once Matthew began talking and bonding with humans, he no longer needed Casper to be his only friend. Their parting worked out well for both Casper and Matthew.

Our son is now fourteen, and he is a Boy Scout and plays baseball. He recently met his biological brother, who is thirty-three years old, and things are going well as they get to know each other. Matthew fondly remembers Casper. That sweet bunny did wonders for my child when he most needed a dear friend. Matthew found a friend with floppy ears and the patience to cuddle him until he was ready to awaken.

Meditation

How have the cycles and changes in life affected your ability to heal? Have different people and animals come and gone with perfect timing?

The Horse Who Heard
Christopher's First Words

....

Kristie Heath, PRAIRIE CITY, IOWA,
and *Deb Hoyt*, RUNNELLS, IOWA

When I stumbled on a healing program that would prove nearly miraculous for my son Christopher, I didn't realize how our lives would change. The program was offered by Healing Hearts with Horses, a new nonprofit organization that had been established at a ranch close to where I live, in Iowa. I learned about it when its volunteers joined the parade during Prairie Days in our town. I knew I had to get in touch with the director, Deb Hoyt, to talk to her about my son.

Christopher had been diagnosed with frontal lobe damage, thinning of the corpus callosum, and autism. At the age of two, he still could not speak, and because of this he was continually angry and out of control. He had his own language, but no one could understand him. The only intelligible word he could say at the time was *no*. He hit, bit, screamed, and threw many tantrums as a result. My husband, Jay, and I had chosen at this point not to use medications on such a young child. We wanted to try natural approaches first, such as horse therapy and homeopathic treatment.

When Jay and I consulted with Deb, she admitted that she had not worked with a child with Christopher's diagnosis. But, she said, "our program certainly will do no harm to your son, and it may help him."

Christopher started weekly sessions with Deb and Snazzy, a beautiful black Shetland pony. Snazzy did not usually work as a therapy horse, but she had chosen Christopher by coming up to him. Deb had learned to listen to the horses when they pick the kids, and to let the kids pick their own horses. She made the right decision to pair these two, because Snazzy was calm and patient with Christopher, which, Deb told us, was uncharacteristic of her. She seemed to understand his needs.

At our sessions with Deb, Christopher's anger would often cause problems. Experiencing new feelings and sensations, he reacted the only way he knew how. One day, Christopher hit Deb in the face and knocked off her glasses. Others who had worked with Christopher got upset with him, but Deb never did. She handled the situation calmly, saying, "Christopher doesn't mean to do those things. It's not his fault. He's angry and frustrated because he can't communicate his needs."

Deb quickly learned Christopher's likes and dislikes and helped to keep him focused. He rode Snazzy bareback, which gives a child the clearest sense of movement on a horse. Since Christopher didn't know that he could fall off, or that he should hang on to Snazzy's mane for balance, Deb had someone walk on each side of him — a sidewalker — to help him stay on the pony.

To hold Christopher's attention, Deb brought a huge bucket of cheese curls to their horse therapy sessions to entice Christopher into playing games with her. Whenever he started to slip into a tantrum, she encouraged him to think about the cheese curls instead. The distraction often forestalled his full-blown outbursts. She called this technique "pattern disruption" and explained that people cannot throw tantrums if they are thinking about something other than whatever made them angry.

Then I made a mistake. At a friend's place, I put Christopher on a big horse and let him ride. After that, he refused to have anything to do with little Snazzy and screamed when we tried to put him on the pony. Deb kept trying, but he would scream, "No! No!"

Deb wanted to get Christopher on a horse again because she

thought this would be the best way to help him. She explained to me that a horse's movements help the child's brain function, similar to the way crawling helps with brain development. The rocking motion also soothes children with sensory issues and calms their emotions. There is no machine that can simulate the movement of a horse. She believed Christopher initially made progress because he had worked with Snazzy, and she was eager to continue their sessions.

It was important for Christopher to work with Snazzy and Deb because, after only a couple of sessions with them, he had already begun talking. He had always verbalized with sounds to let everyone know when he was unhappy, but now he had the use of actual words. For example, he could say, "One, two, three, up," which is what we said when he mounted Snazzy; "Go, pony, jump over the log"; and "Ball, curl" (cheese curl). He was also correctly saying horse-related words, even though he didn't really know what they meant. But he was speaking, and his rapid progress excited us.

Deb and Snazzy

Since we didn't connect my son's new, resistant behavior with the time I put him on a big horse, and we had no idea why he rejected Snazzy, Deb continued to work on the ground with Christopher's sensory issues and to teach him more words rather than stop the sessions entirely. She knew that Christopher did not relate the horse words he said to actions, so she helped him make connections by creating distinctive movements to go with the words. She jumped and said, "Deb, jump." Then she had the pony jump over a log and said, "Snazzy, jump." Finally she had him leap over a log and said, "Christopher, jump." These exercises helped him understand that the word *jump* related to the action of jumping. It was challenging to think of all the words we needed to teach Christopher to relate to actions, but we came up with several exercises that enabled him to improve his comprehension.

We finally decided we were going to have Christopher ride a horse even if he kicked and screamed the whole time. Deb picked Chocolate, an Arabian mare she had brought to her ranch from a kids' camp, to be Christopher's new therapy horse. Snazzy had been a little high-strung, but Chocolate was calm, which Deb thought would make her a good choice.

But instead of screaming because he had to ride a horse, Christopher screamed when we tried to take him off of Chocolate. He wanted the bigger horse. After she saw Christopher's reaction, Deb said, "That makes sense. A child gets more movement from a bigger horse's stride, and more movement helps his brain function better." Christopher had sensed what he needed. He simply hadn't known how to communicate it.

With Chocolate, we were off and running again, and my son was making constant improvements. Christopher was not in school at this time, and Deb continued working with him once a week, from March to October, in an indoor arena to keep up the momentum of his progress. In six months' time, after his lessons with Deb, Christopher was using many words and speaking in full sentences on a regular basis. And, once he could communicate his needs to us, he had fewer tantrums and was much easier for my husband and me to handle.

Deb's fondest memory of Christopher's journey was a moment that happened when they were three months into their therapy together. Christopher often jumped on the trampoline after his lessons — Deb said it helped him release some of the stress of learning new things and eased his transition back into his regular world. On that day, Christopher lay on his belly on the trampoline and put his little hands around his cherubic face. Looking up at her, he said his first full sentence: "I love you, Deb."

Christopher continues to improve. And Deb has never been able to tell that story without bursting into tears.

Meditation

Who have been the human and animal healers who never gave up on you? Are there people in your life who need that kind of patience and consistency from you?

Megan, My Bridge to Normalcy

Jennifer Warsing Hampton, HUNTINGDON, PENNSYLVANIA

Growing up afflicted with a debilitating disease wasn't a kind or normal childhood. My days were filled with solitude, and with pain from being bedridden as Meniere's disease ravaged my balance center and my world spun out of control. This disease is an incapacitating disorder of the inner ear that causes severe vertigo, tinnitus, nausea, and migraines. Sufferers usually lose the balance function of the affected ear, as well as become totally deaf in that ear.

You might think that living day in and day out with an unpredictable and controlling illness would make a child go mad. My saving grace was my best friend, Megan, a collie-shepherd mix, a stray whom my family adopted.

Megan and I were so in tune with each other that she could discern when a severe attack of vertigo loomed, before it struck. Without any special training, she knew enough to force me to lie down wherever I might be. My vertigo attacks could be as brief as a few hours or as long as days. Whatever an attack's duration, Megan would not leave my side — not for food, a drink, a bathroom break, or to play with a toy. Faithful Megan placed my needs ahead of her own.

Depending on what I was doing at the time vertigo struck, Megan would brace herself against me in different ways. If she sensed an impending attack while I was standing or sitting, she would alert me by rooting me with her nose or by gently forcing me to lie down by stretching across my lap or body. If I was in bed and in the midst of an attack, she always stayed beside me on the outside edge of the bed, making sure I was next to a wall. It was as if she knew that, when waves of vertigo struck, I felt as if I could fall off a flat surface.

As the room spun, and I needed to find a sense of center, she would lean against me with the full weight of her body and place her paw in my hands. I would clutch her with all my might, and she would keep her body flush against mine, as if we were one. I would squeeze her paw in fear, wrap my arms around her body and, with her wet nose touching my cheek, hold on during what felt like a never-ending roller coaster ride.

My eyes fluttered during an attack, and I would visually search the room, praying to find an object that didn't seem as if it were spinning out of control. The slightest movement caused the vertigo to escalate beyond what my body could physically tolerate. Megan never moved a muscle while I clutched her for comfort. She would lie facing me, and the first things I would see when my world stopped spinning and my eyes could focus again were her loving, soft brown eyes. After the vertigo subsided, her body would relax, and she would place her head next to mine on the pillow.

Jennifer's Megan

Until the episode passed, it was as if Megan were suffering along with me. She would look at me as if to say, "Friend, I am here." I found consolation and protection in her presence and learned to rely on her for help through each wave of vertigo. Megan knew what I needed before an attack struck, and she tended to my needs during an attack beyond what any human individual possibly could. She was not trained to perform these duties. She was simply an angel in disguise.

Once a bout was over and exhaustion had set in, I would sleep for hours. When I awakened, Megan was always there to greet me, no matter how long my body had needed to recuperate. I spent many hours caressing her soft brown fur and sharing my deepest fears, my wishes for the future, and the joys of the present moment while reading a book, making charcoal drawings, or writing poetry.

I knew my feelings were safe with Megan. She would not judge me, and she loved me for the unique and loving person I was despite my medical condition. During our talks, she showered me with tail wags and with kisses that wiped away my tears and prompted me to squeal with delight, laugh uncontrollably, and feel a sense of peace.

Thanks to Megan and my family's support, my childhood was filled with happy times and love despite my illness. Her companionship and unconditional love gave me normalcy, raised me up from depression, and brought joy when I could find none. She was a blessing each new day, the silver lining in every cloud. Thanks to a collie-shepherd stray, I had the love and companionship of a canine best friend. I may have walked with a poor sense of balance, but I knew that, with Megan in my life, I would never walk alone.

Meditation

Animals don't judge or expect us to be something we're not. If we become the people they believe us to be, we are better human beings. Has an animal seen more in you than you saw in yourself?

PART THREE

....

Compassion

I had a friend; what cared I now
For fifty worlds? I knew
One heart was anxious when I grieved —
My dog's heart, loyal, true.

— AUTHOR UNKNOWN, "My Comforter"

Pepperoni the Turtle
Teaches Jamesey about Change

Paula Timpson, VENICE, FLORIDA

Everyone in my family loves turtles. Our son Jamesey, at age three and a half, discovered sea turtles while watching the *Baby Einstein's World Animals* video. He always smiled when the sea turtle came on. His two favorite colors are yellow and green — turtle colors. I imagine Jamesey one day swimming with the sea turtles or doing work to help them in some way.

Because of our son's fascination, my husband, Jimmy, got us an energetic and wonderful turtle. My mother named him Pepperoni because Jamesey always liked eating the pepperoni slices off his father's pizza.

Jamesey liked Pepperoni the turtle immediately — or Noni, as he nicknamed his new, mysterious, and fun playmate. Jamesey and his turtle reflected each other's pure energy. Noni lived exclusively in the water of his turtle tank, where he loved being fed, and moved quickly to retrieve his food. He played endlessly, racing to the edge of the tank and circling back around as Jamesey ran alongside the tank with him. It appeared that both of them enjoyed challenges and had dreams. After Jamesey learned to feed Pepperoni lettuce by watching my husband, our son, too, started eating lettuce, wanting to be as strong and as good a swimmer as his turtle friend. "Hi, Noni!" Jamesey always said when we came home. "Good night,

Noni," he would say, waving to his turtle friend as our child went to bed.

Jamesey liked to lie on the floor looking up, watching Noni dance and swim in the lighted turtle tank, with its mystical glow. The sound of water flowing in the tank always relaxed our family. Jamesey often fell asleep listening to its gentle, musical rhythm.

Pepperoni liked to climb atop his magical floating rock in the tank. The turtle never gave up, no matter how long it took him to reach the top of his rock. Jamesey was — and is — the same way. He is enthusiastic about life, has great endurance and speed,

Jamesey and one of his turtles

and never gives up. After he sets his mind to do something, he follows through: he invents new things and builds them, catches up on his scooter to the older boys riding their bicycles at the park, or works around the house on his special projects. And like his friend Noni, he embraces water; he's one of the best in his swim class, paddling around like a happy turtle.

When we moved from Long Island, New York, to Florida, we were faced with having to give Pepperoni to some other loving family, because the airline didn't allow turtles on their planes. We introduced Jamesey to a sweet young engaged couple, John and Victoria, who wanted to bring Pepperoni to their home. The couple came to visit us as we prepared to move. They shared their way of life with my husband, and he imagined it would be beautiful for Pepperoni. Jimmy explained to Jamesey that Pepperoni would go with John and Victoria to live with many new turtle and lizard friends in a new, naturalistic terrarium. He told Jamesey that Pepperoni would blend nicely into Victoria's menagerie, a truly wonderful place full of life. Jamesey had to trust that Pepperoni would be okay.

Coping with a big move to a new home far away was on Jamesey's mind. He and Pepperoni would make their new moves at the same time, both surrounded by family and friends. Somehow, this thought made Jamesey more enthusiastic about moving. He was excited because he would have his whole family around him in Florida, and Pepperoni would be with a new family and friends.

When we moved, Jamesey didn't cry, nor was he sad about Pepperoni, because he realized that change is good. It's what makes life wonderful. Since he was a baby, Jamesey's heart has always been very open, and he has never been afraid to try new things.

Today, Jamesey likes living in Florida, where many sea turtles are hatched each year. At the beach, he saw some of the big holes that sea turtles dug in order to lay their eggs. Soon, new sea turtle babies would hatch and head to the ocean. We have talked about how wonderful it is for the baby sea turtles to swim freely in the ocean, which is something Jamesey enjoys too. When at the beach, playing or swimming, our son is very aware that sea turtles live in the water. This makes him feel as if he is touching his friend Pepperoni in his heart, in the sea, and in his memories.

Now we have adopted new turtle friends and brought them into our home. Jamesey, ever strong and growing, watches and enjoys them dancing in the tank, just as he loved to watch Pepperoni. Observing the turtles blissfully munch the lettuce he feeds them prompts Jamesey to eat more lettuce too. When he sees them being still, he lets them teach him to be quiet and tender. As he gazes at them under their heat lamp full of healing, beautiful light, turtles lead Jamesey to peace.

Meditation

Have animals been your mirrors when you had to deal with change? How did they help you find your way to a new home?

Frankie and Jackson
Face Life's Challenges Together

Barbara Techel, ELKHART LAKE, WISCONSIN

··

When I married my sweetheart, John, in 1984 at the age of twenty-one, I thought we were expected to immediately start a family. Unlike so many of my friends and my sister, however, I never desired to have children, and for years I felt as if there was something wrong with me. John did not want children either, but still, my lack of motherly instinct left me feeling odd. It was not until my early forties that I realized God's plan for me was to play a unique role in the lives of many children who were not my own. This welcome discovery came by way of Frankie, my dog with special needs.

My dachshund Frankie was diagnosed with intervertebral disc disease in 2006. When I heard the diagnosis, I was devastated. At the time, I knew nothing about the disease and thought my only option was to put my dog to sleep. But Frankie's surgeon, who removed the ruptured disc in Frankie's back in a one-hour surgical procedure, assured me that if my dog did not walk again, she could still lead a high-quality life in a dog wheelchair. That gave me tremendous hope, though I was still scared, not knowing how I would take care of a handicapped dog. But I loved Frankie so much and knew I had to give her a chance. Every day I am reminded that I made the right choice.

In January 2008 I published my first children's book, *Frankie the Walk 'N Roll Dog*. It is the true story of how Frankie went through physical therapy, was custom-fitted for a dog wheelchair, and persevered. After the book came out, I was scheduled to share our story and do a book signing as part of a fund-raiser in Illinois for Dodgerslist — a membership organization with a website and a quarterly newsletter that supplies information about disc disease in dogs. I wanted to help the organization continue its wonderful work of educating the public about treatable disc disease, which often is viewed as a death sentence for dogs.

The day before the event was to take place, the winds howled and the temperature dropped to thirty degrees below zero. The frigid weather was not expected to let up for two days. The organizer called to say that the event had been postponed until the following Sunday. I was disappointed, since I had been looking forward to it for weeks, but I was also relieved that I wouldn't have to take Frankie out in treacherous weather.

The postponement turned out to be a gift, one that I continue to treasure, because it meant I would be in Chicago later than I'd originally planned, and I could do something important that I hadn't anticipated. A woman named Dawn, who lived in Illinois, wrote me after the event had been rescheduled and said this:

> My sister and I recently stayed at the Osthoff Resort in Elkhart Lake. As we were shopping in the gift shop, I saw your children's book about Frankie. I bought it, hoping it could help my three-year-old son, Jackson. He has hemiplegia, a form of cerebral palsy, and has to wear a brace during the day on his right leg so that, when he walks, his toes and foot do not turn out.
>
> Recently Jackson got a new brace, which he must wear at night to stretch his heel cord when he sleeps. As you can imagine, he dislikes having to wear the brace, because it is uncomfortable.

It is not easy for a young child to understand the reason for wearing a brace. But tonight, after I read Frankie's book to him, Jackson wore his brace to bed without protesting. Frankie's book was a tremendous help. Jackson told me after hearing your dog's story, "I have to wear my brace just like Frankie."

My heart filled with immense joy at the knowledge that Frankie had made such a powerful impact on this little boy's life. At the close of her letter, Dawn asked if we would be in the Chicago area anytime soon. She wrote, "Jackson would love to meet Frankie."

I knew that Frankie and I were meant to meet this exceptional little boy. I emailed Dawn and told her that her letter meant much to me, and how happy I was to hear that Frankie's story was helping Jackson. I suggested we meet at Central Bark, a doggy daycare in Chicago — where the rescheduled Dodgerslist fund-raiser would be held — at two o'clock in the main lobby on the Sunday after Christmas. Dawn emailed back almost immediately. She thanked me and said the meeting time and place I suggested would work perfectly.

Meeting Jackson

It was wonderful being part of the fund-raiser for Dodgerslist and getting together with other pet parents and their beloved dachshunds. I felt inspired to see other dogs living happily with intervertebral disc disease, just like Frankie. And although I was enjoying the event, I could hardly wait for the afternoon, when I was to meet Jackson and his parents.

The time finally arrived. John and I eagerly packed up and waited in the main entrance of Central Bark. We were checking our watches every minute in anticipation, while Frankie busily took in the scents of dog food and dog toys.

Jackson and Frankie

After a few moments, a blond boy came bounding through the front door with his parents, Dawn and Mike, behind him, as well as Dawn's sister, Lori. Tears sprang to my eyes as I recognized the special blessing of this mo-ment. Jackson's smile was in-fectious, and his deep dimples drew me to his sweet face. He was ecstatic to see Frankie and immediately knelt next to her. Lovingly he placed his tiny hand on her back and bent over to look into her eyes. They bonded instantly. Jackson looked up at John and me with his sparkling blue eyes and handed us a doggie doughnut he had brought for Frankie.

Not shy about asking for it, Jackson was eager to take Frankie's leash, which I happily handed over. While he bounced around the main lobby area of Central Bark with his new best pal, Dawn and I looked at each other. Although we did not speak, our eyes clearly conveyed how our hearts felt about the special bond Jackson and Frankie shared because of their challenges.

Jackson took pure delight in playing with Frankie that day. While the two of them were occupied, Dawn showed me the night brace Jackson must wear. She asked, "Can Frankie sign it?" I knew that, with a little help from me, Frankie could. I called her to me and placed her paw in my hand, and together we inscribed Jackson's brace: "Keep on rolling!" I handed Dawn a framed photograph of

Frankie I had brought for Jackson. "I thought you could put this on Jackson's nightstand to remind him he can do anything."

I really didn't want to say good-bye, since I relished all the joy Frankie and Jackson were sharing. But we had a long drive ahead. As we walked out the front door, Frankie snuggled in John's arms. I gave Dawn a hug. Even though our circumstances were different in many ways, they were closely connected because of the special needs we each faced in caring for those we love.

Two days later, another email arrived from Dawn. I could hardly wait to open it. She wrote, "The last two nights, Jackson has put his brace on easily. He asked me to read your book several times and enjoys looking at Frankie's picture and touching her. He now refers to his brace as his "Frankie brace.""

If Frankie Can Do It

Over the next year, I remained in contact with Dawn through emails and her updates about Jackson. She told me that each week he attended physical therapy at a facility in Illinois. Lisa, his therapist, marveled at Jackson's continued progress. She worked with him on strength, range of motion, balance, and movement. In a later phone call with me, Lisa said, "Jackson was so proud to show me his night brace signed by Frankie. After that, everything clicked for him."

Using Frankie as a positive example, Lisa explained to Jackson that Frankie could not walk right away when she first got her wheelchair. But with practice Frankie learned how to walk, run, and play in a new way, just as Jackson needed to do with the brace he wore on his leg during the day. During our conversation, Lisa shared with me that being in an environment at the facility with other children who have challenges, and meeting Frankie, had helped Jackson not to feel so alone in his struggles.

Whenever Jackson resisted learning something new, Lisa would bring Frankie back into the picture as an example of being positive despite challenges. She would explain again that Jackson, like Frankie, had to do things differently. In this way Frankie became a teacher for Jackson, showing him that things are not always easy for her, either. If Jackson became frustrated, Lisa reiterated that Frankie, too, had to practice when she tried new things.

Once the facility where Jackson received therapy learned about Frankie and me, and discovered that I make public appearances and share her story with schools, organizations, and libraries, they asked if I would speak at their yearly winter family event. It was with great honor that John and I, along with little Frankie, made the trip to Jackson's therapy facility on an unusually warm Sunday in January 2009.

When Jackson saw Frankie come through the front door of the therapy facility, he immediately ran toward her. He is a boy of few words, so he said nothing and only knelt down next to Frankie and began petting her. The other children were all waiting in another room, where I would do my presentation. As we walked in, and the children saw Frankie, the room became loud with gleeful shouts: "It's Frankie! Frankie is here!" The children's happiness was palpable.

Pat, the coordinator for the event, introduced Frankie, and I explained how we met Jackson. Before I went into my presentation about Frankie, I thanked everyone for the warm welcome. Then I turned to Jackson and personally thanked him for inviting us to share Frankie's story. He smiled, showing his deep dimples, and quietly said, "You're welcome."

After the presentation, the children eagerly lined up in front of the table for the book signing. One by one, they met Frankie as I signed a Frankie book to each of them. Many children kissed her on the nose, while some hugged her close.

As we left the event that day, I wondered if we would ever see Jackson again. Given the distance and our busy schedule, it's not always possible to arrange visits. But I should have known that the bond between a special boy and a special dog can't be broken and would continue to work its magic.

Jackson's Surprise

The summer of 2010 was winding down when I received an email from Dawn. She said, "I was walking by Jackson's room today as he climbed up on the bed and grabbed the picture of Frankie. So I asked what he was doing. Jackson said, 'Mom, I love Frankie. She was the first dog I ever loved. Isn't she cute? When can we see her again?'"

Dawn told me that, lately, Jackson had seemed to be all about Frankie once again. Even Dawn's sister, Lori, had commented that Jackson mentioned Frankie to her.

As leaves on the trees began to turn shades of crimson red, buttercup yellow, and fire orange, a big day for Jackson was approaching. He would be turning five years old, a special time in a child's life. Dawn was planning a birthday party for him at a local gymnastics facility. As she put an invitation list together, she'd asked Jackson who he would like at his party. Without hesitation he said, "Barb and Frankie."

Not wanting to promise anything to him, she'd told Jackson that it was a long drive from our house to his, and she didn't know if we could come to his party. But wanting to make her son's dream come true, she'd emailed me and asked if there was a possibility we could make it. She said she understood if we couldn't. The request warmed my heart as I thought about sweet Jackson and his love for Frankie. I was happy our schedule was open. And after all, how often does a person turn five years old?

We decided to keep our impending visit a secret from Jackson to add to his excitement. Also, if for some reason we had to cancel it at the last minute, Jackson would not be disappointed. The day could hardly come fast enough. I don't know who was more excited, Dawn or I.

When Frankie and I arrived, Dawn met me outside in the parking lot of the gymnastics facility. I handed her my video camera to give to her sister so Lori could capture the surprise.

When we got to the entrance, I placed Frankie in her wheelchair. I also put a birthday hat on her head that I had made for her two years earlier. With an extra bounce in her step, her head bobbling to the left and right, and her ears swaying, she pranced into the building. It was as if she knew she was on a very important mission.

We found Dawn sitting on the floor with Jackson. She had put a blindfold on him to add to the suspense. As Frankie neared, Dawn helped Jackson to place his hand on the dog's head. She asked, "Who is this?"

As if it could be no other dog, Jackson most confidently said, "Frankie!" He then tore at the scarf covering his eyes to see his special wheelchair friend. I asked Jackson how he knew when he couldn't even see her. He said, "Because it felt like Frankie."

Jackson played with Frankie for a time and then went off to tumble, twirl, run, and just be a boy. He took time out near the end of our stay to once again pose for photos. Then most lovingly he kissed his best pal on the cheek.

As Frankie and I drove home that day, I thought about the time we'd spent with Jackson, and I felt my heart fill with immense joy. I also recalled the early days in my marriage when I'd felt like an outcast for never yearning for children of my own. Having Jackson in my life, as well as the thousands of other children Frankie and I have encountered, has brought the peace that comes from following the path that was meant for me.

Dawn emailed me the day after Jackson's party. On their drive home Jackson had said, "I really loved Frankie being my surprise. I am going to miss her."

The next day Jackson tried on his "I Love Frankie the Walk 'N Roll Dog" sweatshirt we had given him as a gift. His dog, Chance, was sniffing the sweatshirt when Jackson boldly claimed, "Frankie is *my* dog!"

Helping children face challenges can be trying and painful, because we want to protect them and give them the best lives possible. But sometimes we have to give children examples of thinking positively. And if we are lucky enough, we find a special little dog who will silently convey to our children that they can do anything they set their minds to do.

Meditation

Meeting or reading about an animal who handles challenges gracefully and with courage can bring out the spunk in anyone. Do you know a child going through a tough time who would benefit from meeting an animal with special needs?

Reading to Queen Sassy and the Guinea Pigs

Nancy Brooks, MINNEAPOLIS, MINNESOTA

Her name is Sassy, but she prefers to be called Queen Sassy. While her body is small, her royal presence carries enough love to share with all the children she meets. Queen Sassy is my calm, peaceful Sheltie who serves with me in a volunteer program for schools and libraries, the Reading Education Assistance Dogs (R.E.A.D.) program. In 2004, she and I became the first R.E.A.D. team in Minnesota, and Sassy has served as a therapy dog ever since. While on the job, Sassy sits on her blanket and listens as a child reads a story to her. The child benefits from Sassy's nonjudgmental listening and unconditional love. Sassy enjoys the attention and a doggy treat after the child finishes reading a book.

As the human half of the volunteer team, I facilitate an effective interaction between my dog and a child. Quite often, the child will talk directly to Sassy and expect her to enjoy the story. In one instance, when a six-year-old girl sat down to read to Sassy, I introduced them to each other and pointed out that Sassy was wearing a crown-shaped dog tag complete with jewels that formed the word *Queen*. The girl studied Sassy's crown and then carefully selected a book to read to her. The choice that day was a story about Barbie and her friends becoming princesses.

The girl read about half of the book. Then she stopped and whispered to me, "Is Sassy the queen of all dogs?"

After pausing to savor the thoughtfulness of her whispering such a sweet question, I answered, "Why, yes, Sassy is the queen of all the dogs in my house."

The little girl resumed reading to Sassy. After several more pages, she stopped again and asked, "Does Sassy have a king?"

"Of course! My dog Dandy is the king of all the dogs in my house."

Katie reads to Sassy

I realized after hearing her questions that the child had chosen a book about Barbie as royalty because she thought Sassy would like it. While she read to an audience of one dog, she had been thinking about how the book related to what Sassy's life must be like.

Reading to Guinea Pigs

While dogs are the most common therapy animal partners involved in R.E.A.D., the children are always delighted to see a guinea pig, too. This type of small animal can be less intimidating to a child who might be hesitant to approach a dog. Some kids are surprised to learn that a guinea pig will sit and listen to them.

My guinea pig Cocoa Puff has listened to a lot of stories in his life. One girl spent quite a bit of time searching for the right book to read to him. She selected a rhyming book, *Smooch Pooch*, because she knew Cocoa Puff would like it.

After a few minutes of listening to her story, Cocoa Puff started nosing around inside his little fabric nest, a cozy cup where the guinea pig stays while the child reads to him. With one little finger the girl gently scratched the distracted guinea pig's head, and he immediately turned around to look at her. She said, "When you look at me, you can hear the story better."

One day, a nine-year-old boy asked if it would be okay to read a book that was written in Spanish to Jelly Bean, another R.E.A.D.

Nancy's Cracker Jack and Cocoa Puff

guinea pig. I said that this would be a great idea, since Jelly Bean likes learning new things. It would be the first time anyone had read to him in Spanish, so, I told the boy, I thought he would enjoy the experience.

I asked the child if he could also tell the guinea pig what was happening in the story. The boy read a page and then showed pictures in the illustrated book to Jelly Bean. He explained the meaning of the story in great detail. Reading took about one minute per page. Describing the story and translating it from Spanish into English took five minutes for each page. The boy stayed focused on making sure Jelly Bean understood and could appreciate the story.

Over the years, I've observed that R.E.A.D. goes beyond helping a child improve his or her reading skills. It is much more than a cute thing to do. After participating one-on-one with a R.E.A.D. animal for as little as a few weeks, fifteen to twenty minutes each time, children show a remarkable increase in self-esteem, improved self-confidence, better attendance at school, and more involvement in school activities. All this is accomplished with the help of animals who pay attention and listen.

It Takes a Dog to Calm a Child

One time, a social worker asked me if I could spend some time with "Sharon," a ten-year-old girl who was severely afraid of dogs. Her phobia had begun when she was younger and a Sheltie had chased and cornered her. She had screamed until someone came and took the dog away.

After a few years, her parents decided to seek professional help for their daughter. Her fear of dogs had increased to the point that it severely impaired her ability to relax and enjoy life. She was always afraid that a dog might appear nearby and frighten her. And Sharon's anxiety was negatively influencing her younger brother's attitude toward dogs.

The social worker did therapeutic exercises with Sharon to help her learn how to remain calm around dogs. They discussed her options for responding to the sight of a dog and rehearsed how to interact with one. They were at a stage in the therapy when the child was ready to be exposed to a dog in a controlled setting.

Sharon's mother and I decided to first introduce Sharon to one of my guinea pigs. By starting with a guinea pig instead of a dog, the child would more easily get to know me and accept my animal partner. I selected Rudy, a perfect gentleman. As Sharon got used to Rudy's presence, she began to feed him carrot slices and eventually began to pet him. She was thrilled with the success of that first session.

In our next session we introduced Sharon to my Sheltie Sassy. We did a series of sessions with different interaction techniques. Initially, we had Sharon sit on one side of me, with Sassy on my other side, and we talked about Sassy. To be so close to a dog was a very big step for her. Sassy must have sensed this because she lay serenely next to me.

During the next visit, Sharon took the big step of sitting next to Sassy. In subsequent visits, she progressed to brushing Sassy with a long-handled brush, a small brush, a palm-held brush, and then to finally actually petting her. In a short time, she became comfortable around Sassy. This was a remarkable achievement, considering that the catalyst for her dog phobia had been an aggressive Sheltie.

After Sharon became relaxed around Sassy, we introduced her to my other therapy dog, Ali, a five-year-old Sheltie. Ali was well mannered, but Sharon had to adjust to the younger dog's movements, which were much quicker than the older Sassy's. However, we soon started showing off all the tricks Ali could do. Sharon was quite impressed that she could get Ali to spin in a circle, take a bow, and crawl. She enjoyed being with the more actively responsive, energetic dog.

It was heartwarming to see Sharon's interactions with Sassy and Ali. Her confidence improved, and she no longer fled when a dog happened to come near her. At the beginning of one session, her mother and I were discussing what to do next, since it seemed Sharon had reached a plateau. At that moment, the girl spontaneously started walking Ali without waiting for me to hold the other end of the dog's double leash. Her mother and I were both thrilled to witness the sweetest childhood image — a young girl happily skipping with a beautiful dog by her side. The two of us had tears in our eyes at this significant breakthrough.

We went on to introduce Sharon to dogs of different sizes, breeds, colors, and energy levels. She accepted them well. It was clear that our therapy visits were no longer required when she declared that she wanted a dog of her own.

All the animals in my life have brought such joy with their personalities and their love. To share these wonderful beings with children has been a true blessing for me, for the animals, and most of all for the children.

Meditation

Would you like to try letting a child read to a dog or another animal who sits quietly and listens? When have you welcomed a good listener who never told you that you got it wrong?

Unbreakable Willow

Meaghan Martin, HOLLIS CENTER, MAINE

When the sad little golden pony first arrived at the camp and riding-lesson stable where I work, she was unnamed and underweight. We only knew that she was in her late teens and had birthed too many foals. She had ended up in a kill pen with a colt at her side. A kill pen is a section at an auction designated for horses who are destined to be purchased by a kill buyer and shipped to Canada, where they will be slaughtered for horsemeat. Some horses are fortunate enough to be purchased by outside sources and given another chance at life. Such was the case with Willow.

After her brush with death at the auction, Willow went to live in a private home and became a backyard therapy pony for a person who had a child with disabilities. My boss isn't sure where Willow went after this home, but right before she came to our stables my boss's father bought the pony. He had been told that she would be great as a beginner-lesson pony. He had also been promised that she would be safe as a walk, trot, and canter mount for our more advanced students, who could learn to do these things on her.

Willow was thin and had to gain weight. But I was head over heels the moment I met her. Her golden buckskin coat was a sweet, beautiful color, similar to Willow's equally sweet disposition. The dusting of snowflake spots across her rump — an homage to the Appaloosa blood in her — signaled that she was a member of the Pony of the Americas breed. Sadly, she bore marks of a painful past. A scar ran jaggedly across the white stripe on her face. A wart-like lump on her lip remained from a once-deep cut that had not received the stitches it needed. A chunk was missing from her otherwise smooth neck, where she must have been sliced by a wire. A golf-ball-sized hard lump protruded next to the cannon bone on her left front leg.

The little mare's conformation was awful. Her back was too long and swayed deeply from the stress of carrying foals. Her neck looked as if it had been put on upside down. Her hips were far higher than her shoulders, making her look as if she were standing on sloped ground, with her rump higher than her forehand. Some people said that her scars and conformational flaws made her ugly. But to my way of thinking, she had survived so much and those scars were proof of her will to keep going. Despite all her imperfections, I instantly thought she was the most beautiful creature I had ever seen.

I thought painstakingly about a name that would suit the little golden pony. She had bent in the windstorms of her life, but had not broken. She needed a name as special as she was. I was delighted when my boss approved the name I carefully selected for the new mare: Willow.

After Willow gained weight, our senior instructor had to evaluate her under saddle. The young woman stepped into the stirrup and swung up onto Willow's back. As she rested the weight of her body on Willow, the mare exploded and jumped straight up and down. Her back hunched tightly underneath her rider, and the instructor came tumbling off to meet the dusty arena floor.

Rumors flew around the stable about how the "crazy mare" had thrown the instructor. Several staff members believed that she was dangerous and that we should get rid of her. But I dared to believe that Willow needed someone who would listen to her and try to figure out what she was thinking. Instead of just pushing Willow, I wanted to figure out why she was behaving this way. Maybe then I could work with her to overcome the obstacles created in her past.

A couple months later, we discovered during a routine veterinary visit that Willow was actually twenty-four years old. She had quite a bit of soreness in her withers, which are located where her neck, shoulders, and spine connect. Though this would not typically have affected her soundness under saddle, a person putting weight in the stirrup would pull against the withers. When the instructor had mounted Willow, it had caused significant pain. A rider placing the saddle farther back and not using the stirrup when mounting could lessen the pony's reaction.

The instructor had taken neither of these precautions, simply because we were unaware of Willow's condition. Now armed with the new information, another staff member was given permission to ride the pony. Willow accepted being mounted, until it came time to canter. Then she bucked like a bronco. The rider stayed on her, but it did not look good for the pony. She was older than promised, and she could not adequately perform the skills we had been told she possessed. She would have to go back to my boss's father's farm. We didn't know what he would want to do with an old, crazy pony. If he sold her because of her age and lack of usefulness, things would not look good for her.

I was crushed by the news of Willow's imminent fate. I truly loved this little pony and related to her. The cruelty of mindless people had left physical scars on my body, too, in the form of self-mutilation. Other students attending my high school had not been kind to me. I had left the painful past behind, but my skin still bore the scars of plentiful, self-inflicted wounds. I had had little confidence in myself and no reason to believe or trust in people. Like Willow, I had been betrayed and hurt.

Anyone who has been a cutter, the vernacular for someone who mutilates herself by cutting her skin, knows the intense, emotional, and unavoidable turmoil that accompanies the practice. Cutting leads to a vicious cycle of shame, depression, and self-doubt. I had somehow made it through those vulnerable teenage years. Now Willow and I were two scarred survivors, stranded together and unsure of where we would go from there.

I pleaded with my boss to let me try to rehabilitate the little pony, and she gave me an ultimatum. It was mid-July. I was to have Willow ready to serve as a walk-, trot-, and canter-lesson horse by the end of the summer, or the pony would have to leave our stables.

Earlier in the summer I had worked with a four-year-old filly who had had no experience with being ridden. I treated Willow in the same way that had been successful with the other horse. I assumed nothing. I made everything slow and clear and was always quiet and gentle. I decided to start by using pressure so slight that Willow would hardly be able to feel it. If she did not respond, I would gradually increase the pressure and immediately decrease it when she accepted it. I would always give the mare a chance to do things the easy way, with as little resistance as possible.

Willow and I connected immediately while I was in the saddle. With the pressure-release system I used, she was able to understand me and respond appropriately while I was on her back. But she had a lot to learn. She understood neck reining, a style of steering used only in Western-style riding, in which the horse is ridden on a loose rein and steered with one hand instead of two. With Western-style neck reining, the horse responds to the pressure that the reins exert on the side of the neck simply by lying against it. If the rider lifts her hand and moves the reins to the right, putting pressure with the rein on the left side of the neck, the horse moves away from the pressure and to the right.

We teach English-style riding, which uses different gear, including a smaller, lighter-weight saddle. The rider uses two hands to steer instead of one. One of my first priorities for Willow was to teach her to respond to this direct-rein style. With English-style direct-reining, the rider applies gentle pressure by pulling the rein that faces the direction she wishes to go, which turns the horse's nose in the direction of travel.

For example, if I wanted to ask Willow to turn right, instead of lifting the left rein and putting it up against her neck, which is what she already knew how to do, I had to teach her that if I gently pulled on the right rein, I wanted her nose to turn to the right and the rest of her body to follow. The two types of steering are nearly opposite to each other, and switching a horse from one to the other can be difficult and frustrating.

In addition, Willow needed to strengthen her back muscles. This would alleviate her soreness and allow her to canter without pain or other difficulty.

We worked together three times a week, and each session strengthened our bond. Willow never gave me any attitude, which ponies are notorious for exhibiting. Instead, she worked as hard as I did.

I loved seeing how smart she was. Granted, Willow still needed to build muscle and stamina to maintain her canter. Also, she had a difficult time picking up the correct lead. When horses canter, they lead with one of their front feet. In order to help them maintain balance when they are being ridden, they are asked to lead with the foot that is on the same side as the direction of travel. If Willow cantered to the left, I would want her to lead with her left front leg. Horses have a strong side and a weak side, and Willow was stronger on the right. Since her cantering muscles were not strong yet, she always wanted to lead with her right foot when cantering, even when we were going left, and this affected her balance. She learned to lead with the correct foot in about two weeks — so quickly that I knew we would accomplish my goals. We cantered as if she had been able to do it all along.

Our stable sponsors an informal horse show at the end of the summer so that campers or students can gain show experience while riding familiar horses in a nonthreatening place. The week before the show, I put a student on Willow for the pony's debut as a lesson horse. The boy loved Willow so much that he begged me to let him show her.

The next day, another student had the same pleasant experience with Willow. We decided that she was ready to let students ride her in the show. The other staff members knew that I had essentially adopted Willow, and they let me bathe and braid her when I arrived on the morning of the show. I felt as proud of her that day as I was of my students.

Willow competed in five classes of varying difficulty, from lead line class, in which the rider is assisted by a handler who helps to control the horse by attaching a lead line to his or her bit, through walk-trot-canter classes, in which the rider competes independently by showing the horse in each of the gaits. Willow brought home several ribbons. Our mission was complete. She had proven herself to be incredible.

I continue to work with Willow to further her training and strengthen her back. Her scars have not disappeared, and her neck still looks like it's upside down, but her swayback is less pronounced because her back is stronger. I gave a student a walk, trot, canter lesson on her, and she was as steady and predictable as she always is with me.

Meaghan's Willow

I always look forward to riding Willow, because it is a freeing experience. When we work in sync, there is no room for negative thoughts to invade my mind. All that exists is here and now, in this place, with this one golden pony. Willow has shown me that believing in something or someone is not a bad thing. I believed in her when no one else did, and she chose to work with me. Not once did she threaten to buck, rear, or do anything else dangerous. I knew we could trust each other.

One night after a workout, I stood in Willow's stall, whispering in her ear about the people who had hurt me. I explained to her that I have scars too and understand how the things people do and say can cut deeply. Willow listened quietly and let me love her.

When I call to Willow while she is in the field, her head raises, her eyes shine, her ears prick up, and she marches toward me, plainly happy to see me. She has helped me to heal in so many ways. And she has lived up to her namesake, never letting anything break her. Willow has scars, but she does not let them define her, nor does she allow her physical flaws to limit her. She is beautiful just as she is.

If Willow can let storms shape her, if she can again trust humans, if she can overcome her past, maybe I can too. It's been said, by an unknown author, that "all horses deserve, at least once in their lives, to be loved by a little girl." The reverse of this sometimes rings truer: all little girls, at least once in their lives, deserve to be loved by a horse.

Meditation

Has having compassion for an animal, child, or adult enabled or increased your ability to heal? Have beings come into your life at exactly the right time to give what you need?

Rescued Dalmatian, Sparkles
the Fire Safety Dog, Rescues Others

Dayna Hilton, CLARKSVILLE, ARKANSAS

She has red toenails, a red vest, an official firefighter badge, and a tail that wags nonstop. My Dalmatian, Sparkles the Fire Safety Dog, also has a mission. Together, she and I help save lives, reduce injuries, and decrease property losses from fire. Sparkles, rescued from a home with sixty-two dogs, has reached millions of children and their caregivers with fire safety messages since my family adopted her in May 2003.

Sparkles loves children, and I believe she was destined to be a fire safety dog. On the day my husband and I met her, we were at a large adoption event held by the Dalmatian Assistance League of Tulsa at a pet supply store. After we were introduced to her, we took four-year-old Daisy (later renamed Sparkles) into the store so we could walk around and get better acquainted with her. I noticed that she was immediately drawn to children shopping with their parents. When she voluntarily lay down to let children pet her belly, I knew she was the dog for our family.

Sparkles had been rescued from deplorable living conditions. I couldn't deal with knowing more about the miserable life she had led, and wanted to look forward, not backward. It wasn't until seven years after adopting her that I was emotionally ready to learn more about her history. Sparkles's most recent home had been with a representative from the Dalmatian Assistance League. She explained to me that Sparkles had previously lived with a man who rescued dogs and apparently had become an overwhelmed animal hoarder. The conditions inside the man's house were described as horrible. The City of Tulsa Animal Welfare agency rescued Sparkles and the man's other dogs. Later the league agreed to take all the Dalmatians, including Sparkles.

The representative from the league believed that living with the animal hoarder had not traumatized Sparkles, and that "her spirit had never wavered." She said that Sparkles was fortunate because she had not needed rehabilitation, and that throughout the entire rescue process her tail had always wagged happily. That was the Sparkles I knew. The representative also stated that quite a few of the rescued dogs had not been so lucky; some had been traumatized by what they'd experienced. I was saddened to hear this story and to think of all these less fortunate dogs.

Sparkles's Journey

In 2000, soon after I became a volunteer firefighter, I decided to focus on helping to save young children from fire by teaching fire prevention. According to *The Fire Risk to Children*, a report by the United States Fire Administration and National Fire Data Center, 20 percent of fire deaths occurred in the fourteen-and-under age group. The report also noted that data compiled for 2001 by the National Center for Health Statistics indicated that fire deaths in that age group were up by 15 percent.[1] After realizing the enormity of these statistics, I developed a program that was not only educationally sound and fun but also lifesaving.

After adopting Sparkles in 2003 with the sole intention of making her a member of our family, I soon realized that she was a fast learner and enjoyed going with me to the fire station. She loved interacting with the other firefighters. One evening, just for fun, I wanted to see if Sparkles could "crawl low" for me. This is a key fire safety behavior that I was teaching children as part of my program. In a building on fire, the air is cleaner and cooler twelve to twenty-four inches from the floor. "Get out" and "Go to our family's meeting place" are also instructions that parents must give their children for fire safety in the home. With a video camera in one hand and a treat in the other, I asked Sparkles to crawl low for me. It was exciting to watch her follow the command on her first attempt.

I realized then that Sparkles could be my partner in fire safety education. Demonstrating other fire safety behaviors also came easily for her. She would jump into her bed when I directed her to do so. I would cover her with a blanket, and she would pretend to be asleep. At the sound of a smoke alarm she'd jump out of bed, crawl low, and go to the meeting place I'd designated.

Sparkles Helps Save Lives

One of the most touching moments in our fire safety careers came when I learned that Sparkles had helped save the lives of two children and their two families. Sparkles and I had visited Tulsa, Oklahoma, to read from our book *Sparkles the Fire Safety Dog* and make a fire safety presentation for approximately 450 pupils at Celia Clinton Elementary School. Each child that day received the book, courtesy of the Rotary Club of Tulsa.

The school's principal, Mrs. Tanya Davis, emailed me about two months later and asked me to contact her. She added that I should have a box of tissues handy when I called. The thought kept racing through my mind that one of her students had died or was injured by fire. To my relief, when we spoke on the phone she told me that two children at her school had been involved in fires over the Christmas holiday, but that the outcomes had been good.

Mrs. Davis related the experiences of both children, Angelica Riggins and Dystiny Hodges, and later Angelica gave me her story in her own words. About Dystiny, the principal told me, "I was walking down the hallway, when one of my third graders came running up and said, 'Mrs. Davis, my microwave caught on fire, and I grabbed my brothers and sisters, and we got out of the house, because we saw smoke.' Dystiny took a breath, and then said, 'Sparkles taught us to get out quick, so we ran outside.'"

At that moment, I knew Sparkles and I should have a follow-up visit with the students. I could not let this teaching moment pass.

Angelica and Sparkles

It was my duty as a fire safety educator to reinforce the fire safety message. And I couldn't wait to meet Angelica and Dystiny, the students who had helped to save their families' lives because of what Sparkles had taught them.

I ended the phone call with tears of joy in my eyes and ran to hug Sparkles. Not one, but two saves. I couldn't breathe. I realized for the first time that we really were making a difference.

During our follow-up visit to the school, five-year-old Angelica told me her story. She said, "Firefighter Dayna, I was in bed under the *cubbers*, and the smoke came. I crawled out of bed and crawled low, just like Sparkles showed me. I said, 'C'mon, Daddy, you have to get on the floor and crawl low like Sparkles.'"

Angelica's dad had become disoriented while standing in a smoke-filled room in the burning house. Fortunately, he was able to follow his daughter out. The responding firefighters later told me that, as soon as Angelica's father reached the door, they had scooped him up and taken him to the hospital. He spent seven days there, four in the intensive care unit. The firefighters said that the home had flashed over, which means it became totally engulfed in flames, just as they got Angelica's father out the front door.

Every day, I think of Angelica and Dystiny and am thankful that Angelica and her dad, and Dystiny and her family, are alive and well. Knowing that Sparkles and I made a difference in their lives is gratifying. It inspires me even more to make children fire-safe.

Sharing the Fire Safety Message Around the Country

When Sparkles got older and could no longer travel as much, we began conducting Skype visits with schools throughout the United States and around the world. Skype allows the fire safety dog and me to make fire safety presentations live via the World Wide Web, which classes can view by computer. In our present economic environment, schools have experienced deep budget cuts and are highly interested in Skype as a venue for sharing fire safety messages.

Another effective means I have used to bring fire safety to children is my selection of books featuring Sparkles. All are educationally sound and based on the latest fire safety practices presented in *Fire Safety for Young Children: An Early Childhood Education Curriculum*, published by the Oklahoma State University.[2]

Sparkles and I also worked with the twenty-four-hour preschool channel PBS KIDS Sprout. The program's website features fire safety videos, games, activity sheets, and other no-cost materials. Over the years, numerous national magazines, websites, and television programs have featured Sparkles and her fire safety demonstrations for children. She was awarded the title Most Heroic Dog for 2010 by *USA Today*.

In May 2008, we added a new member to our fire safety team, another Dalmatian, named Tango. Siren, a Dalmatian puppy, also joined our family and fire safety education team, adding his talents to our effort to keep more children and their caregivers safe. And in 2009, I started the nonprofit Keep Kids Fire Safe Foundation to continue the mission that Sparkles and I began.

I could not have asked for a more amazing partner than Sparkles. She touched so many lives over the years. I truly believe that she found her calling, and I am grateful for the blessing of having her in my life.

Meditation

Sparkles instantly connected with children and helped to keep them safe. Could what you were meant to do in life have something to do with enriching, and even saving, the lives of children?

Brut, My Brown-Eyed Boy

Linda M. Johnson, ESKO, MINNESOTA

Love at first sight is real. It happened to me when I was not quite nine years old. Maybe I shouldn't have fallen so hard, so fast. A love that strong can only end in heartache. But I couldn't help it. At the time, I lacked warmth in my life, and finding someone who openly showed me affection instantly secured him a place in my heart.

The first time I looked into his deep chocolate-brown eyes, a feeling of peace and happiness came over me. We connected. While holding him, my heart filled with the long-lost joy I never thought I'd experience again. I didn't want to let it, or him, go. Immediately I loved him unreservedly. I knew he loved me too. Maybe it was women's intuition maturing early in me, but I knew.

From the moment he curled his lips up in a goofy dog-smile and wagged his entire body, he made me smile from the inside out. His puppy-dog eyes gazed at me with adoration. He was black on his back, had a black headband above his eyes, and was honey-gold everywhere else. His fur felt warm and soft to the touch when I'd stroke his ears or scratch his belly. It was literally puppy love I felt for Brut, my brown-eyed boy.

Before I met Brut, I was a lonely little girl. It hadn't always been that way. But one cool Sunday morning in the fall, when I was eight years old, my mother died. Shockingly. Unexpectedly. My world forever changed. The messages I'd been given in Sunday school had been about God's unconditional love, but to me, heaven was still an abstract concept. My source of unconditional love was gone.

Oh, how I missed my mom. Not only was she gone forever, but also my dad was not the same loving, happy man. Now that I am an adult, I can look back on that time and honestly say I don't blame him for drowning in grief. Losing his wife at the age of thirty-six must have been heart wrenching. Even now, with a spouse of my own, I can't begin to imagine the pain he experienced, because I haven't suffered the devastating loss of a partner. However, I don't think he realized the extent of my anguish either. No one did. Although only my mother died, it was as if I had lost both parents that cruel October day.

I hid my pain well. I rarely, if ever, talked about my mother's death. Instead, I internalized the pain, holding it close inside. Years later, I discovered the freedom of expressing loss through writing and sharing. Yet as a small child, I thought the unspoken rule was not to dwell on loss and to get on with life. There were no grief counselors. I did the best I could under the circumstances.

More often than not, I comforted my father, instead of the other way around. There were times I'd find Dad in the living room, desolate, with his head in his hands. He'd sit in the nubby brown chair that mom had preferred because she could swing her legs up over its side and relax while reading one of her many books. I'd hug Dad and say it would be okay. I didn't really think it would be, but I lacked any other words. At the age of eight, I didn't have the vocabulary or insight to assure a grown man that the hurt would fade. I didn't know that, although memories could not replace Mom, they would give all of us solace in the years to come.

Sometimes late at night, the sweet release of slumber would be elusive as I listened to the sound of Dad's sobs filtering through my bedroom door. I'd bury my head under my pillow, and tears would run down my cheeks, soaking my sheet and mattress. I often prayed and cried myself to sleep, rocking in the bed, holding a worn, striped, stuffed cat that was now pinned together. Mom wasn't there to sew my toys anymore; safety pins replaced her patient stitches.

Then the day came when Dad met a woman. He didn't cry anymore. When I met her, she introduced me to the brown-eyed dog her family called Brut. They had named him after the aftershave her adult sons always wore. The dog spoke to my soul. I didn't have any objection when Dad married the lady, because Brut got to live at my house. It seemed only natural that I was more excited about the dog than the lady or her kids who came along with Dad's new marriage.

Linda and Brut

We lived out in the country, and I didn't have neighbors nearby to play with. Counting my older brother and sister and the stepchildren inherited after Dad remarried, I was the youngest of ten. The oldest siblings had moved away from home; a couple of them had jobs. Since all of them were older than I, they weren't around much. And besides, they were too cool to play with me, their littlest sister. Dad and his new wife were wrapped up in each other. Alone most of the time, I felt invisible, as if no one knew I existed. But it was okay. Brut knew.

Brut and I roamed the woods. Sometimes we'd follow well-worn cow paths that led to my grandparents' farm. Or Brut would accompany me into the nearby meadow, where I'd pick bouquets of daisies, buttercups, and black-eyed Susans. When the season was right, I'd search for tiny wild strawberries while Brut rested in the cover of tall grasses. In the winter he'd patiently trot beside me as I tobogganed down and trudged back up the small hill behind our house. We were always outside together somewhere. Brut's dog-house was big enough that I could climb inside with him and shut out the reality of my changed life.

Brut listened to me when no one else did. He knew my secrets and fears. More than once, he sat patiently while I hugged him. Sometimes I'd cry, and he'd lick the tears from my cheeks. Brut was not man's best friend. He was my best friend.

Because he couldn't come to school with me, Brut waited at the end of the driveway until the bus pulled up, and he watched me get on it. Every day when I arrived home, he ran to meet me, his back end swaying from side to side and tail wagging enthusiastically. His lips curled up, baring his teeth and giving him his trademark, silly smile. He smiled mostly for me. He liked everyone else, but loved me best. Of this, I had no doubt.

As the human years passed quickly, so did the seven-year dog years. Time took its toll on Brut. His steps grew stiff and arthritic. Even though he smiled and wagged his tail, the aches and pains of aging limited his enthusiasm. The veterinarian said Brut was fine; it was just old age. But he reminded us that we shouldn't expect our dog to live forever. Even his muzzle was turning white, giving him the look of the wise old man I knew he was.

One day, I came home from school, and Brut wasn't there to greet me. It was the first time since he had moved to our house that he hadn't met me with his smile at the end of my school day. His water bowl and food dish weren't in their usual place. I knew. He was gone.

Once again, I internalized the loss and couldn't bring myself to talk about it to anyone. Instead, I cried silently in my room. Though I was nearly grown and ready to leave my childhood home, I'd still spent a lot of time outdoors with Brut when I could. He'd always made me smile, no matter how bad my day had been. After he was gone, roaming the woods lost its appeal, and my interests turned to other things. Nothing was the same anymore. With adulthood almost upon me, I felt like a lonely little girl again.

It has been many years since Brut left this world. A special dog, he brought love back into the life of a small girl to an extent I think no one but I could ever know. Puppy love is real love, no matter what grown-ups say. I'll never forget my beautiful brown-eyed boy.

Meditation

Children dealing with death, divorce, and blended families could use a compassionate friend like Brut. Are there ways for you to bring an animal's special kind of caring into the life of a hurting child?

Bella Made Me Forget the Bullies

Lisa McMurtray, CENTRAL FLORIDA

I am eleven years old now, but one morning when I was in third grade, I was walking to class and not bothering anybody. Suddenly, a boy named "Kaden" ran up and for no reason punched me in the stomach. It hurt badly and felt so terrible that I threw up in front of everybody.

I was in a crowded place where everyone was trying to get to class. Kids moved past me, rushing to get away from the trouble. Some kids laughed and pointed. I hurried on to class.

Later, in the cafeteria, I overheard a few fifth-grade kids calling me Puke Face. It made me feel really bad to think that the entire school might know about me throwing up, and it hurt my feelings that kids were laughing at me. Back in homeroom, some girls, who were not my friends, whispered and looked my way. I knew they were pleased that I was having such a rotten day.

Three hours later, I was at the gate to Freedom Ride stable looking forward to a weekly riding lesson with my favorite bay quarter horse, Bella. I brighten up when I get to be with Bella, because she is familiar to me. She is seventeen years old and always calm. I grabbed a helmet and ran to find her. I was so relieved to see her.

That day, I hugged Bella's neck and breathed in her scent of sweet hay and cherries. I love helping to get her ready to ride, because when I brush her it calms me and makes her shiny.

I put Bella's hackamore headgear on her and clipped on a lead rope. Then I led her out and brushed her down thoroughly as I told her about my day. It felt good to be able to let out what had happened at school. I felt so embarrassed about the whole thing that I hadn't even told my mom about it. I know I can tell Bella anything, and she will listen. She loves me and never lectures or laughs at me. I love her because she comforts me. I feel like I have known her for a long time.

Lisa and Bella

Bella nuzzled my cheek and snorted, trying to tell me to forget about the bad times. Next, I put on her saddle pad. I wanted to feel connected to her, so I chose not to use a saddle that day. Riding Bella makes me feel free and independent. As I clipped the reins, I felt that she knew what I was feeling and how to make it better. I jumped up on her back and settled in. I was home and where I belonged.

As we started moving together, I wondered how Bella always could tell what I was feeling. I knew that she had helped me just by being herself.

Meditation

Bullies come into our lives at all times, not only in childhood. Has an animal's kindness and attention turned your bad day around?

A Dog Named Leaf Knows
Where the Ow-ees Are

Allen Anderson, MINNEAPOLIS, MINNESOTA

My dog, Leaf, and I have our Saturday rituals. I tell our all-black cocker spaniel that Saturday is a day of great adventure and fun. One of the best parts of Saturday occurs when I drive Leaf to the dog park near a city lake. This park is about an acre of bumpy ground with a few scruffy chairs where people sit to watch their dogs play.

I repeatedly throw Leaf's precious orange ball, so he has plenty of playtime and running. After he tires, we sit and relax on a large, hollowed-out log and watch the other dogs and their humans. They are a study in the amusing ways canines and people relate to each other. In my opinion, people tend to reveal their personalities by how far and often they throw balls or Frisbees for their dogs. And who retrieves the ball or stick — the person or the dog — says a lot about their relationship. Leaf and I discuss the different dogs — which ones are nice; which ones play too roughly.

About a year earlier, my wife and I adopted Leaf from an animal shelter that had a sign on his stall identifying him as "Abandoned." After he came home with us, we were surprised by how deprived he had been. Clearly he had never lived inside. Even more poignant was the fact that he showed signs of never having had a toy of his own. When he went to a pet supply store, and we let him pick out his first stuffed, long-bodied, squeaky toy dog, he brought it home and wouldn't part with it. He took the dog everywhere and slept with his little arms wrapped around its body and his head resting on the soft toy's head. The sound of his little toy squeaking sent him into ecstasy.

After the visit to the dog park, we always go to a small local pet supply store to buy the very best dog, cat, and bird food. Our bird, Sunshine, gets new millet and a complete cleaning of his cage that day. I bring home new kitty litter for the cats, Speedy and Cuddles. The boxes of dog treats at this store are kept at floor level, and they turn Leaf into a brazen shoplifter. Because the place is a smell-fest, loaded with toys and food dogs love, Leaf is beyond excitement as the car approaches the parking lot. He bounds out the car door, pulls on his blue leash, hurtles his body into the store, and flits from one welcome sight or smell to another. He runs his large black nose along the row of dog toys and rifles through buckets of chew bones. He sniffs, explores, and enjoys every moment.

One Saturday morning, Leaf and I were in the aisle that had anti-itch spray products for the cat. I was reading ingredients while Leaf poked his nose into each toy, apparently to discover which ones squeaked the loudest. For a dog who had only a year ago possessed his first toy, this section of the store was a corner of heaven.

A ten-year-old boy with tousled Scandinavian-blond hair and curious blue eyes came up and asked if he could pet Leaf. I said, "Yes, but he might not want to play. He's on a mission to find the perfect toy."

Even though he was still hyper from the nearness of so many goodies and distracted by them, I guided Leaf over to the boy. He kept one eye on the toys, lest some other dog get the idea to invade the territory he had staked out. Leaf stayed only long enough for the boy to give him a quick pat on the head. Then, bedazzled by the nearness of so many goodies, he rushed back to continue his exploration.

I told the boy that Leaf was excited to be in the store. The little

Allen's Leaf

fellow's face sagged, and he unexpectedly looked too sad and tired for someone his age. He spoke quietly and said, "My dog died yesterday."

I could have responded to his words in many ways. But looking at the sorrow etched on his young face, I sensed that right then, he needed only empathy, not an adult conversation about dealing with pet loss. I gently and simply said, "It must hurt a lot."

The little boy replied, "Yes, it does." He added that his dog had died of cancer and lost any awareness of where he was at the end.

Leaf stopped poking his nose at the squeaky toys. Nothing distracts this dog from a good toy hunt, but now he seemed to be listening as the grieving child spoke about his dog. The animal had been his companion, his buddy. They went together everywhere. The dog slept in his bed at night. Nothing was or ever would be the same without him.

Abandoning his earnest search for a perfect squeaky toy, Leaf looked thoughtful. Then without any prompting from me, he walked back to the boy. Leaf normally does not like to be near little children, because they are unpredictable with their actions and movements, and he craves predictability. Children might want to squeeze him too hard or tug at his floppy ears.

I remained quiet while Leaf sat still in front of the boy. He seemed to sense that he could comfort the grieving child by letting him pat him on the head. This time, he stayed longer, focusing his dark brown eyes on the child's face as the boy petted him and scratched behind Leaf's ears. After a few moments, Leaf moved away but did not rush back to the toys. Instead, he matched the child's somber mood by making his gait slower as if he were mirroring the boy's emotions.

The boy looked up at me. The sparkle in his eyes revealed that the empathic presence of our healing little cocker spaniel had silently lifted the burden of loss from his heart. He said thank you and went back to his parents.

I looked at Leaf who had returned to his toy search with more focus and not quite as much gusto. I resolved to buy the toy of his choice for my little guy with the big heart. He had forgiven our species and learned to love and trust the humans in his new home. Having known sorrow, Leaf, with his act of kindness, made me think that he understood the little boy's loneliness and had tried to alleviate it in a way that only a cute little cocker spaniel could.

Leaf keeps his secrets to himself, so I don't know exactly why he does things such as what he did for the grieving child. My belief is that a loving animal like Leaf is an instrument of the Divine. Someone's heart is broken, and Spirit directs a creature with a wagging tail, soft fur, sweet eyes, and a kind heart where he's most needed.

Meditation

When empathy emanates from a creature with furry paws, the healing effect can be breathtaking. Has an animal helped you or a child release a burden of loss?

Afterword

I need so much the quiet of your love
After the day's loud strife;
I need your calm all other things above
After the stress of life.

I crave the haven that in your heart lies,
After all toil is done;
I need the starshine of your heavenly eyes,
After the day's great sun.

— CHARLES HANSON TOWNE, "At Nightfall"

Magic happens when the right animal and the right kid get together. An animal never judges, never scolds, never makes a little one feel anything other than big. Kids grow up. Animals grow old. Although an animal's physical presence fades, a child never forgets wiggling up against a furry body or having the undivided attention and devotion of a being who listens to secrets and keeps them safe.

The child is in charge of the animal-kid relationship, or so it appears. But the stories in this book show how animals, with their quiet, voiceless, highly effective ways, protect and nurture kids in need. Animals support children with tenacity, creativity, and grace, whether by offering a temporary intervention — entering quietly and leaving swiftly — or by permeating a home with their presence.

And then there is the thrill of meeting someone who has no agenda other than to give love. How often does that happen? Or the thrill of getting up close to a farm animal when you have only seen its kind on television.

We hope that reading *Animals and the Kids Who Love Them* has given you some great ideas about how and why to do whatever you can to enrich children's lives with an animal presence. Even if it's offering time or money to support organizations that are dedicated to serving children and caring for animals, you will have contributed to one of the most beneficial relationships on earth.

Children have read and been told fables and other stories about animals for thousands of years. It is inconceivable to think of childhood without animal friends — real or imagined. When children can touch, hold, and talk to an animal, the experience carries them to a world where all things are possible. When a child has the friendship and loyalty of a pet, it becomes a foundation for self-love and self-confidence. Children follow the paw prints of a childhood pet right into adulthood.

Listen to your heart when a child asks to interact with an animal. As much as we all need to be careful when pairing children with pets, or putting a child around an animal we don't know, there comes a time and a place when this act of kindness is exactly what we have to do. Animals make children whole. They speak to kids in ways that grown-ups and other children cannot equal, imitate, or exceed. They charm children from dark caves of loneliness. They play with them when no one else has the time or interest. They love them with each breath until the end of the animals' lives.

What more could you ask of a friend, companion, and golden playmate?

What to Consider When Deciding to Bring a Pet into the Family

....

Interview with *Sonia C. Velazquez*

We spoke with Sonia C. Velazquez, former senior vice president of the American Humane Association. The team she worked with specializes in child protection and advocacy. We asked her to give some pointers on how to carefully bring a pet into a home with children.

Allen and Linda: For those who aren't familiar with the American Humane Association, can you explain more about the organization?

Sonia: The American Humane Association promotes the positive potential of the human-animal bond and has developed a scientific approach that demonstrates the benefits of this relationship. In general, the organization works intensely to develop skills in professionals and agencies, based on evidentiary practices, so that both children and animals flourish. The organization also develops specific programs to advance the well-being of children and of animals and examines how these two are connected. The goal is for this connection to be a part of the staff's everyday perspective when they think about how to protect the most vulnerable among us.

The American Humane Association encourages the education of social-work professionals and caseworkers — in the development of tools and family assessment procedures — to look for signs of animal abuse and neglect, which can be an indicator of a lack of family resources, including those that promote child safety and well-being. Doing so ensures that all members of the family get the crucial help that they may need. In issues of neglect, the American Humane Association advocates the practice of looking at the entire situation, including how pets may be impacted by a family's breakdown.

Allen and Linda: What do parents need to consider in planning for the addition of an animal family member?

Sonia: Rather than surprising a child with a pet as a gift, which can have disastrous results for both the animal and the family, have conversations and communicate with the child.

Consider questions such as these:

- Does the child like animals, and how has the child responded to neighbors' or family members' pets in the past?
- Has a parent talked with the child about having a pet, and about the amount of time, energy, and resources it takes to care for animals?
- Does the child understand that the pet must be treated with respect, kindness, and patience at all times?
- Does the family have space for a pet in its current housing situation?
- Is the home safe for a pet?
- What is the family's financial situation in regard to pet food and veterinary care?
- Does the family have access to training for any pets?
- At this stage of the child's development, what animal would be the best choice for a pet?
- Do the animal's needs and the family's needs match? Are they a good fit?

More Factors Related to Pets for Children

Answering Sonia's thoughtful questions, and looking at how well matched your child's personality would be with a pet you are thinking of adopting, can help you avoid falling into the trap of making a hasty, emotional decision about bringing an animal into the home. Many animals who have been given as "gifts" wind up in shelters or become strays roaming the streets. Such an outcome would not be a good lesson for a child to learn about how to treat an animal, and certainly it would not be good for the animal.

Another reality of giving a child a pet is that parents have to get ready for the fact that children don't always follow through on their promises to feed, groom, and spend time with the animals they insisted on having. These are optimal teaching moments but can also be sources of frustration for harried parents. In the *Wall Street Journal*, Jeff D. Opdyke wrote of his reservations about getting a pet for his seven-year-old daughter, who had begun asking for one. His first reaction was to say no. The family was busy with daily chores. He had to travel a lot. His wife, Amy, would have one more obligation. But then he started remembering the animals who had shaped and enriched him. "Pets, at least for me, were an integral part of childhood. And I realized that to understand my daughter's desire for one, I needed to stop thinking like Dad and start thinking like the pet-loving kid I used to be."[1]

To help in the selection of the right pet for a family, a clever and research-based method for matching was designed by Kenneth Dagley, a trainer, and Dr. Jacqueline Perkins, a veterinarian from the GOOD DOG Behaviour Clinics in Australia. Their Canine Behavior Type Index provides a personality analysis of dogs to determine their temperamental traits. The index measures three dimensions of personality: level of organization, social position in a hierarchy, and energy level. After a person figures out a dog's classification, there are twelve profiles that guide him or her in handling dogs with certain personalities. The test is available for free at www.petconnectgame.com.[2]

Acknowledgments

With respect and love, we give our appreciation to Georgia Hughes, New World Library's editorial director, who has worked with and encouraged us to bring to the world the messages in *Animals and the Kids Who Love Them*.

We are grateful to the wonderful visionary Marc Allen; marketing director and associate publisher Munro Magruder; our enthusiastic and amazing publicity director, Monique Muhlenkamp; managing editor Kristen Cashman; type designer Tona Pearce Myers; cover designer Tracy Cunningham; copyeditor Bonita Hurd; proofreader Lindsay DiGianvittorio; editorial assistant Jonathan Wichmann; and the rest of the staff at New World Library.

We sincerely appreciate the encouragement from Harold and Joan Klemp, who inspired us on our journey of giving service by writing books about the animal-human spiritual bond.

We are so blessed to have Robin Ganzert, PhD, president and CEO of the American Humane Association, and the incomparable Steve Dale, a board member for the organization as well as a syndicated columnist and radio host, write the foreword for this book. We have great admiration and respect for all that the American Humane Association does to help children and animals. We especially want to thank Sonia Velazquez, the organization's former senior vice president, for the insightful interview she gave us for the book. And thank you Shannon Peterson, former philanthropic services officer, corporate relations, for making everything flow so smoothly in order for us to support the American Humane Association.

Our deep gratitude goes to Al Peterson, executive director of Can Do Canines of Minnesota for all his help in finding and editing the story "Midas Makes Our Dream Come True," which depicts the organization's amazing contributions to people with disabilities.

A special thanks to all the incredible contributing authors who shared their stories in this book about cherished experiences with the healing and loving relationships between animals and children.

We greatly appreciated the wisdom and generosity of the judges of the 2010 Animals and Children True Story Contest: Jodi Buchanan and Marcia Pruett Wilson. The contest became a rich resource for many of the stories in this book.

We extend our heartfelt gratitude to Stephanie Kip Rostan of Levine Greenberg Literary Agency, Inc., our energetic literary agent. She had the wonderful idea for the theme of this book and helped us from its inception to its finish.

We also thank members of the Saturday Morning Minnesota Screenwriter Workshop sessions led by Chris Velasco for all the support and affection. The Loft Literary Center continues to be a beacon and haven for writers, like us, and we are grateful for our relationship as teaching artists with this outstanding organization. Special thanks to the Thursday Night Writers group and PetPAC (Pet Professionals and Companies), a networking group for pet business owners and nonprofit organizations in Minnesota.

Our families instilled a love of animals in us at an early age. We especially appreciate Allen's mother, Bobbie Anderson, and Linda's mother, Gertrude Jackson. To our son and daughter, Mun Anderson and Susan Anderson: you're the best. Much love to Allen's sister, Gale Fipps, and brother, Richard Anderson, and their families.

Special thanks to Darby Davis, editor of *Awareness* magazine, for publishing our column, "Pet Corner," all these years, and to Kathy DeSantis and Sally Rosenthal for writing consistently beautiful book reviews. To Lessandra MacHamer: you have always been in our corner, and we love you for it.

And thanks to our current animal editors, Leaf, Speedy, Cuddles, and Sunshine. Without you, we wouldn't have been able to fulfill our purpose.

Notes

Introduction

Epigraph: Emily Marshall Eliot, quoted in Katherine C. Grier, *Pets in America: A History* (Chapel Hill: University of North Carolina Press, 2006), p. 73.

1. American Pet Products Association, "Industry Statistics and Trends," 2011, www.americanpetproducts.org/press_industrytrends.asp (accessed February 1, 2011).

2. Hal Herzog, *Some We Love, Some We Hate, Some We Eat: Why It's So Hard to Think Straight about Animals* (New York: Harper, 2010), p. 81.

3. Gail F. Melson, *Why the Wild Things Are: Animals in the Lives of Children* (Cambridge, MA: Harvard University Press, 2001), p. 29.

4. Tanja Hoff and Reinhold Bergler, "The Positive Influence of Dogs on Children in Divorce Crises from the Mother's Perspective and of the Child-Dog Relationship from the Child's Perspective" (presented at the "Ninth International Conference on Human-Animal Interactions, People and Animals, a Global Perspective for the 21st Century," Rio de Janeiro, Brazil, September 13–15, 2001, www.deltasociety.org /Document.Doc?id=36 (accessed February 1, 2011).

5. Jennifer Christiansen, "History of Animal-Assisted Therapy," September 24, 2007, www.associatedcontent.com/article/385777/history_of _animalassistetd_therapy.html?cat=72 (accessed February 1, 2011).

6. Ibid.

7. Aaron H. Katcher and Gregory G. Wilkins, *The Centaur's Lessons: The Companionable Zoo Method of Therapeutic Education Based Upon*

Contact with Animals and Nature Study (Tucson, AZ: Animal Therapy Association and People, Animals, Nature, 2002).

8. "Program Description," 2011, Our Farm website, www.ourfarmschool .org/description.php (accessed February 1, 2011).
9. Michele A.Woellner, email message to the authors, December 20, 2010.
10. Grier, *Pets in America*, p. 27.

Part One. Hope

Epigraph: Jalal al-Din Rumi, "The Long String," in *The Essential Rumi*, translated by Coleman Banks with John Moyne, A. J. Arberry, and Reynold Nicholson (New York: HarperSanFrancisco, 1995), p. 80.

Part Two. Healing

Epigraph: "Marvelous Cures at Epidaurus," *American Antiquarian and Oriental Journal*, ed. Stephen Denison Peet (Chicago: F. H. Revell, 1884), p. 304, http://tinyurl.com/3q887fp (accessed April 1, 2011).

Part Three. Compassion

Epigraph: June Cotner, ed., "My Comforter," in *Dog Blessings: Poems, Prose, and Prayers Celebrating Our Relationship with Dogs* (Novato, CA: New World Library, 2008), p. 72.

1. United States Fire Administration and National Fire Data Center, *The Fire Risk to Children*, Topical Fire Research Series, vol. 3, no. 8, December 2004, www.usfa.dhs.gov/downloads/pdf/statistics/v4i8.pdf (accessed May 31, 2011).
2. Kimberly Simmons Coates, Jamie Johnson, Margaret Napier, and Shannon White, *Fire Safety for Young Children: An Early Childhood Education Curriculum* (Stillwater: Oklahoma State University Fire Protection Publications), http://imis-ext.osufpp.org/imispublic /Content/NavigationMenu/RESEARCH/FireSafetyForYoung ChildrenCurriculumDownloads/default.htm (accessed April 2, 2011).

Afterword

Epigraph: Charles Hanson Towne, "At Nightfall," in *The Best Loved Poems of the American People*, ed. Hazel Felleman (1936; reprint, New York: Doubleday, 2008), p. 52.

Appendix

1. Jeff D. Opdyke, "The High Price of Pets. But So Worth It," *Wall Street Journal*, December 26, 2010.
2. Pet Connect, www.petconnectgame.com (accessed April 19, 2011).

Contributors

Barbara L. Babikian, "Lille Is an Angel on a Leash." Barbara Babikian has been a court stenographer for twenty years, and she lives on five acres with her husband of twenty-four years and her four dogs, including Lille. Barbara and Lille have been featured on the Animal Planet channel twice, on other television shows, and in newspaper and magazine stories. Lille has a modeling career that includes a Ralph Lauren photo shoot and an Alpo ad with Taye Diggs. She's been photographed in the arms of Cesar Millan, Vera Wang, David Frei, and Jill Rappaport. But Lille's most important work and number one job will always be as a furry friend for someone who needs a loving dog to hold and hug. Learn more about Angel on a Leash at www.angelonaleash.org, about Delta Society at www.deltasociety.org, about the Ronald McDonald House at www.rmdh.org, and about New Alternatives for Children at www.NacKidsCan.org.

Nancy Brooks, "Reading to Queen Sassy and the Guinea Pigs." Nancy Brooks enjoys a lifelong love of reading and of dogs. She was astounded when she discovered that the two passions could be combined, and that she could actually take her dog to the library. In 2003 Nancy created a therapy-animal visiting program at a local animal shelter. She cohosted the first therapy animal conference in the Twin Cities in 2005 and hosted the Reading Education Assistance Dogs (R.E.A.D.) national conference in 2010. Nancy attributes the majority of her success to her wonderful partner, Sassy. When Nancy and Sassy aren't reading in schools and libraries, Nancy is a project manager with a financial services company. For more information about Reading Education Assistance Dogs, visit www .therapyanimals.org/R.E.A.D.html and www.READdogsMN.org.

Carolyn C. Corbett, "Justice for Children with Golden Caitee." Carolyn Corbett is founder and executive director of K9 c.a.r.e.s. Victim Support, a nonprofit 501(c)3 organization that uses animal-assisted therapy to assist child and adult victims of crimes. After assisting the victims of the Columbine High School shooting, Carolyn tirelessly worked to construct the K9 c.a.r.e.s. Victim Support program. She was one of the few civilians who received a police service ribbon from the Jefferson County Sheriff's Department for her work at Columbine High School on April 20, 1999. She lives in Colorado with Philip, her husband of twenty-two years, and their three therapy dogs, Caitee, Tallulah, and Liberty. Tallulah joyfully assists children with their reading. Liberty was handpicked to follow in Caitee's paw prints as an advocate K9. At only one and a half years old, she is a registered therapy dog working at the University of Colorado Hospital and in the Reading Education Assistance Dogs (R.E.A.D.) program at the Westminster College Hill Library. Visit www.k9cares.org for information.

Thuvan DeBellis, "A Cat Therapist for David." Thuvan DeBellis lives in Jacksonville, Florida, with her husband, two daughters, and David. She currently teaches fifth grade and enjoys the challenges and successes she encounters each year. Portions of Thuvan's story were first published as "Baby's Teacher Is a Cat!" July 7, 2010, in *Pet Tips 'n' Tales*, an online newsletter by Mary Ellen Angel Scribe.

Nanci Falley, "Childhood Horses Saved My Life." Nanci Falley is founder and owner of Rancho San Francisco in Lockhart, Texas, where she rescues abandoned and abused animals. Since 1979, she has owned and been president of the American Indian Horse Registry (www.indianhorse.com), dedicated to the preservation of the original horses of Native America. The organization had its fiftieth anniversary in 2010.

Linda Freedman, "Peter Pan's Nana Became My Daughters' Playmate." Linda Freedman is a freelance writer living in Connecticut. Her articles have appeared in the *Angel Animals Story of the Week* newsletter and in *Best Friends Magazine.* She has two daughters, Erica, who is thirty-three years old, and Emily, who is twenty-eight. All of Linda's pets are rescues. BooBoo is a shepherd cross; Moe is a very fat, gray, shorthaired cat; Ziggy is a black-and-white tuxedo cat; and Roxy is a tabby with cerebellar hypoplasia. Linda continues to volunteer with local rescue groups and has fostered more than one hundred cats and kittens. Her website is www.lindafreedman.org.

Judy Fridono, "Surf Dog Ricochet Changes the World for Children." Judy Fridono is founder of Puppy Prodigies, a nonprofit organization that focuses on early puppy development and service dog training that prepares dogs to help people with disabilities. See www.puppyprodigies.org/Welcome.htm. She also has a website devoted to her fund-raising projects involving her dog Ricochet, which contains video clips, photos, and news stories that have been viewed by millions around the world. See www.surfdogricochet.com. Ricochet has over twenty thousand fans on Facebook, who are incredibly supportive; see www.facebook.com/SurfDogRicochet. Patrick Ivison's website is www.helppatrickwalk.org.

Kristie Heath and **Deb Hoyt,** "The Horse Who Heard Christopher's First Words." Kristie Heath and her husband, Jay, have four boys, all of whom have special needs. The couple keeps very busy coping with their children's medical issues. Deb Hoyt is executive director of Healing Hearts with Horses and Horse Heaven Equine Rescue. She provides equine-related therapy and more at her little farm in Runnells, Iowa. She depends on the general public for donations to operate her nonprofit organizations, since most families who need therapy do not have the means to pay for it. Learn more at hhhiowa.com and horseheaveniowa.org.

Dayna Hilton, "Rescued Dalmatian, Sparkles the Fire Safety Dog, Rescues Others." Dayna Hilton is founder of the nonprofit Keep Kids Fire Safe Foundation. The foundation's goal is to help save lives, reduce injuries, and decrease property losses from fire by developing and distributing educationally sound, innovative fire safety–related materials at little or no cost to children and their caregivers, fire departments, schools, and other organizations, as well as by presenting fire safety programs. Sparkles and Firefighter Dayna have been featured in numerous publications, including *Cesar's Way, Dog Fancy, Dog World, DogSport, FIDO Friendly, American Dog,* and *Parent* magazines. *Sparkles the Fire Safety Dog* and *Sparkles Goes to Boston* are multi-award-winning, critically acclaimed children's books. See Sparkles sharing the fire safety message on www.sproutonline.com/firesafety and at www.sparklesthe firesafetydog.com. On October 26, 2010, Sparkles passed away, but she left behind a legacy of helping to save children's lives.

Linda M. Johnson, "Brut, My Brown-Eyed Boy." Linda M. Johnson lives in northeastern Minnesota with her family and their adopted dachshund mix. Her writing has been published in various publications. In 2010 she won the Northwoods Woman Fiction Contest and saw her first memoir published. She savors small pleasures such as dark chocolate and a good cup of coffee.

Ellie Laks, "The Turkey Who Helped a Blind Teenager Find Her Song." Following a dream she'd had since the age of seven — of

bringing rescued farm animals and troubled children together —
Ellie Laks founded The Gentle Barn, a nonprofit 501(c)3 corpora-
tion, in 1999. Ellie and Jay Weiner, who joined forces with her in
2002, now run it. Each of the 130 farm animals has been rescued
from horrible abuse, neglect, and loneliness, and yet all have survived because of their courage and their ability to forgive, trust, and
love. These are the qualities that Ellie and Jay strive for daily and
which they teach to the children who visit The Gentle Barn. The
organization is frequently featured on *The Ellen DeGeneres Show*,
and it welcomed a televised visit from Ellen and Portia DeGeneres
in 2010. Learn more at http://gentlebarn.org.

Meaghan Martin, "Unbreakable Willow." Meaghan Martin is
studying English at the University of Southern Maine. She has four
incredible horses of her own and considers Willow an "adopted"
member of her equine family. When Meaghan is not in class or
writing, she can often be found engaging in another passion, photography. It should not come as a surprise that her favorite subjects
are the horses who have given her so much. Meaghan also had a
story, "Charlie, the White Marble Statue Healer," published in Allen
and Linda Anderson's book *Horses with a Mission* (New World
Library, 2009).

Lisa McMurtray, "Bella Made Me Forget the Bullies." Eleven-year-
old Lisa McMurtray lives with her family in central Florida. Her
hobbies include horseback riding, swimming, reading, speed skat-
ing, watching television, and annoying her brother. She dreams of
being a contestant on the PBS television show *Fetch! with Ruff Ruff-
man*. Lisa plans to become a herpetologist.

Miriam Palevsky, "Casper the Rabbit Touched My Son." Miriam
Palevsky and her husband, Marvin, have been married for twenty-
five years and have six children. They were foster parents for twenty

years and rescued rabbits for many years. They support the rabbit rescue organizations Michigan Rabbit Rescue (www.michigan rabbitrescue.org) and the Buckeye House Rabbit Society (www.ohare .org). Visit the Palevsky's website at www.mybunnies.com, and contact Miriam at webmaster@mybunnies.com. For pictures of Matthew and Casper, go to http://mybunnies.com/casper.htm.

Diana Richett, "Simon, My Cat with Special Needs, Gives Hope to Children." Diana Richett is a lawyer in Colorado, currently in private practice, who represents children as a defense attorney in delinquency cases and as a guardian ad litem in child abuse and neglect cases. She is a founding director of the Colorado Juvenile Defender Coalition and a certified veterinary technician. She is the proud guardian of Simon and other special-needs dogs and cats. Since 2009, she has partnered with her cat, Simon, and her three-legged dog, Tiva, in the American Humane Association Animal-Assisted Therapy program. Through this program, she tutors children for the University of Denver's Bridge Project at the Westwood Opportunity Center in the Westwood Housing Projects in Denver, Colorado. Learn more about the American Humane Association Animal-Assisted Therapy program at www.americanhumaneaat.org.

Tom Russo and **Peggy Frezon,** "Miniature Horse Patty Pat Answers a Parent's Prayer." Tom Russo is a physician's assistant who loves skiing and woodworking and happily reports that Patty, the miniature horse in his story, had a foal named Avatar. Peggy Frezon is a pet columnist and author of *Dieting with My Dog* (Hubble and Hattie, 2011). Her work appears in *Guideposts* magazine; more than a dozen Chicken Soup for the Soul books, including *Chicken Soup for the Dieter's Soul* and *Chicken Soup for the New Mom's Soul*; and other publications. Visit Peggy's Pet Place, www .peggyfrezon.blogspot.com.

Mona J. Sams, "Missy's Magical Llamas." Mona Sams, MA, OTR, is the founder of Mona's Ark in Roanoke, Virginia. She is a seventy-two-year-old occupational therapist with over forty years of experience in developing and implementing therapy for children and adults with special needs. Mona and her innovative animal-assisted therapy approaches are featured in DVDs produced by the Latham Foundation, Animal Planet's *Animal Miracles*, and a Canadian television station, all of which are available at Mona's Ark, www.monasark.org. Mona is eager to help others replicate her methods for providing occupational therapy by incorporating llamas, alpacas, and other animals in order to achieve established therapeutic goals. Email Mona at creativetherapycare@gmail.com.

Barbara Techel, "Frankie and Jackson Face Life's Challenges Together." Barbara Techel is the award-winning author of *Frankie the Walk 'N Roll Dog* book series. Barbara and Frankie regularly visit schools and libraries in Wisconsin, and elsewhere via Skype. They routinely volunteer as a certified therapy dog team at local hospitals, nursing homes, and hospice centers. Frankie has been named a Wisconsin Pet Hall of Fame Companion Dog. Learn more about intervertebral disc disease at www.dodgerslist.com. Visit Frankie's website at www.joyfulpaws.com.

Pam Thorsen, "My Child with Autism and the Dog Who Adores Her." Pam Thorsen and her husband, Dick, are innkeepers and owners of the Thorwood and Classic Rosewood Inns in Hastings, Minnesota. Their interests are historic preservation, ecotourism, sustainability, and animal welfare. They are happy to live in Hastings, home of Animal Ark, a no-kill shelter, as well as the Carpenter Nature Center, an amazing and nurturing nonprofit organization that promotes the welfare of animals and nature. They have another daughter, Tiffany, who owns a dog-walking business in Santa Cruz,

California. Like her parents, Tiffany is happy to live in a town with excellent animal humane societies, but she also has sunshine and the ocean. Contact Pam at www.thorwoodinn.com or email her at pam@classicrosewood.com.

Paula Timpson, "Pepperoni the Turtle Teaches Jamesey about Change." Paula Timpson has written poetry and stories since she was young, and she creates in celebration of God's glory. She loves to share her poetry ministry with the world. Paula has an MA in special education and believes everyone has potential. Writing is a fulfilling part of her life, and her son, Jamesey, is her muse. Visit Paula's website, http://paulaspoetryworld.blogspot.com.

Jennifer Warsing Hampton, "Megan, My Bridge to Normalcy." Jennifer Warsing Hampton is employed as a kennel technician at the Huntingdon County Humane Society. In her spare time, she enjoys participating in educational programs with her hearing dog, Hattie, as ambassadors for Dogs for the Deaf (www.dogsforthedeaf.org). Jennifer is also a member of the fund-raising committee for her local animal shelter. She enjoys writing short stories, making pottery, and cooking. Her story in this book was winner of the Angel Animals Network's 2010 Animals and Children True Story Contest.

Tanya Welsch, "The Kindness of Horses, Llamas, and Chickens." Tanya Welsch, MSW, LICSW, is a licensed school and independent clinical social worker. For over twenty years she has provided therapy and learning programs involving animal-assisted interactions. She is the founder and director of the nonprofit Natural Connections Learning Center, and she consults for the University of Minnesota's Nature-Based Therapeutic Services Program. Contact her at tanya.welsch@gmail.com or www.naturalconnectionslc.org.

To learn more about the Children's Country Day School, go to www.childrenscountryday.org.

Julie Yanz, "Midas Makes Our Dream Come True." Julie Yanz lives in Minneapolis, Minnesota, with her husband, Craig; children Maddie, Zachary, and Matthew; and dogs Jasper and, of course, Midas. Can Do Canines pairs assistance dogs free of charge with people who need them. For more about autism assistance dogs or other canine helpers, visit www.can-do-canines.org.

Additional Photographers

Except for the following, the photographs accompanying the stories in this book were taken by the contributors.

Page xii: Photograph by Anne Grant — the Village Photographer, www.grantphoto.com, Clemmons, North Carolina. Copyright © Anne Grant. All rights reserved.

Page xiii: Photograph courtesy of Tribune Media Services and Steve Dale. All rights reserved.

Page 12: Photograph by Anna Bjorkstrand, Anna Bjorkstrand Photography, Minneapolis, Minnesota. Copyright © Anna Bjorkstrand. All rights reserved.

Page 21: Photograph by Robert Ochoa, San Bernardino, California, www.PawMazing.com. Copyright © Robert Ochoa. All rights reserved.

Page 24: Photograph by Tamandra Michaels, San Diego, California, www.heartdogstudios.com. Copyright © Tamandra Michaels. All rights reserved.

Page 73: Photograph by Sandy Clark, Andover, Minnesota, www.addictioncounselor.org. Copyright © Tanya Welsch. All rights reserved.

About Allen and Linda Anderson

....

Allen and Linda Anderson are inspirational speakers and authors of a series of books about the physical, emotional, and spiritual benefits of having pets as family members. In 1996 they cofounded the Angel Animals Network to share stories that convey uplifting messages about the relationships between people and animals.

In 2007, their book *Rescued: Saving Animals from Disaster* won the American Society of Journalists and Authors Outstanding Book Award. In 2004, Allen and Linda were recipients of a State of Minnesota Certificate of Commendation in recognition of their contributions as authors. In 2011, they were named Partners and Friends of the American Humane Association in recognition that their mission and efforts are in alignment with the organization's work.

The Andersons' work has been featured on the *Today* show, the *ABC Nightly News*, *The Montel Williams Show*, and the Animal Planet network, as well as in national wire service articles, magazines, and newspapers, including *USA Today*, the *Washington Post*, *O Magazine*, *Best Friends Magazine*, *Dog Fancy*, *Cat Fancy*, *Fido Friendly*, and *Animal Wellness*, among others.

Allen Anderson is a writer and photographer. He was profiled in Jackie Waldman's *The Courage to Give*, a book that was featured on *Oprah*. Linda Anderson is an award-winning playwright as well as a screenwriter and fiction writer. She is the author of *Thirty-Five Golden Keys to Who You Are & Why You're Here*. She is a board member for a networking group of Minnesota pet businesses and nonprofit organizations, PetPAC. Allen and Linda teach writing at the Loft Literary Center in Minneapolis, where Linda was awarded the Anderson Residency for Outstanding Loft Teachers.

The Andersons share their home with a dog, two cats, and a cockatiel. They do fund-raisers for animal rescue organizations and donate a portion of revenue from their projects to animal shelters and animal welfare.

You are welcome to visit Allen and Linda's website at www .angelanimals.net, and their home pages and groups on Facebook (search "Angel Animals" and "Animals and the Kids Who Love Them") and Beliefnet (Angel Pets Fan Club). They invite you to send them stories and letters about your experiences with animals. At the Angel Animals website or by email, you may also request a subscription to their free email newsletter, *Angel Animals Story of the Week*, which features inspiring stories about animals around the world.

Contact Allen and Linda Anderson at:

Angel Animals Network

P.O. Box 26354

Minneapolis, MN 55426

Website: www.angelanimals.net

Email: angelanimals@aol.com